EVA SZYBALSKI

LWÓW - A CITY LOST

MEMORIES OF

A CHERISHED CHILDHOOD

if eBooks - P. Moeller

First edition published 2015
ISBNs:
Mobi   978–3–945093–20–7
ePub   978–3–945093–22–1
Print   978–3–945093–21–4
Printed in the world

if eBooks - P. Moeller
www.if-ebooks.de

ACKNOWLEDGEMENT

The following people gave me the benefit
of their individual contributions

Waclaw Szybalski
Basia Sandor-Hunter
and
Ezra Weisman.

I am also grateful to my paternal grandparents

Stefan and Michalina

without whom this book could not have been written.

This book is dedicated primarily to my cousins

Jola, Basia and Stefan

DEDICATION

It is also dedicated to

Jul Szybalski

and all those who are curious about how this man, who plays such an important role in our lives, was shaped, and actually born with his unabashed straight-forward honesty which until today remains refreshing, at times startling, but also often very funny.

Especially when he comments on his own actions.

Thank you, Daddy.

Contents

PROLOGUE

I, Stanislaw Zygmunt Szybalski, was born on December 18, 1927 in Lwów, Poland.

These are my childhood memoirs. Due to the fact that I am writing my memoirs more than 80 years into my life, my memories are not infallible. So, I ask you, dear reader, to please excuse me, if my story may be somewhat ambiguous.

Following are the memories of my childhood that may be influenced by time and are today tainted by an adult's mindset.

In my attempt to insure maximum accuracy, I compared my recollections with my brother Wacek (Wacław) who is six years older than me. During the process, I began to realize that although he may have a more mature perspective of my childhood, his memory might not be as focused as mine. Consequently, acknowledging that, although two contemporary witnesses are better than one, it doesn't ensure total objectivity of events past. Unfortunately, I cannot compare my memories with many of the other people who shared moments of my life, because they are no longer among us.

Taking this compromise into account, I will try to recount the story of my childhood in Lwów from 1927 to 1944 as accurately as I can.

1. WHERE IT ALL BEGAN

Some people say that life begins with our birth. In my case, the first momenta of my potential existence occurred in 1925, two years before I was born. The root of my being arose from the tragic story that befell the Czekanowski family.

Professor Jan Czekanowski was an internationally renowned scholar of African ethnology and a physical anthropologist who taught at the Jan Kazimierz University (UJK) in Lwów. Even today he remains famous, earning himself a lasting place in the history of the social sciences as an eminent scholar of African anthropology and as the creator of the Polish school of anthropology. His wife Liza Czekanowska was a physician from Russia and spoke with a heavy Russian accent.

PUPPY LOVE

The Czekanowskis were very close friends of my parents. They spent their summer vacations together in Brzuchowice, a summer resort in the outskirts of Lwów.

The most memorable holiday was in the summer of 1925. My brother Wacek was four years old and totally devoted to Zorka, the Czekanowski's only child. Whether the 9-year-old girl liked him because she harbored maternal feelings or not, we'll never know. In any case, the two children were best friends and inseparable that summer.

Wacek and Zorka in 1925

TRAGEDY IN THE O.R.

Life took a brutal turn when Zorka was rushed to the hospital one day with acute appendicitis. This required surgery and the attending physician gave her chloroform as an anesthesia, which in those days was common practice. But something went terribly wrong during the operation, and the chloroform killed Zorka.

Mrs. Czekanowska, who was present in the O.R., was so devastated, she nearly went berserk and smashed every piece of glassware she could get her hands on in the operating room.

Zorka, Dziadek Tadeusz Rakowski and Wacek, 1925

TO BE OR NOT TO BE

The loss of Zorka had a great effect on my parents. Their interpretation was that if you had only one child, and that child was taken from you, your entire world would completely collapse.

That's when they decided to have a second child. And the tangible result of that idea became me.

Wacek Szybalski

My Father

My Mother

2. (1927–34)
SAINT MAREK STREET
NUMBER TWO

MY HOMETOWN

I came into this world on December 18, 1927 in Lwów, Poland. For centuries, my hometown has been inhabited by people of different ethnic backgrounds and therefore has had many names: Leopolis (Latin), Lwów (Polish), Lemberg (German), L'vov (Russian), L'viv (Ruthenian or Ukrainian) and Lvov (English).

Lwów is situated at the crossroads of important trade routes linking the East with the West and the South with the North. Benefiting from its strategic location, Lwów rapidly developed economically, especially in the second half of the nineteenth century.

Under the reign of the Austro-Hungarian Empire at the end of the 18th century, Lwów's prominence as the capital of Galicia had been attracting intellectuals from all walks of life. Jews, elsewhere persecuted in Europe, were welcomed to Poland and especially to Lwów, also called "Paris of the East".

As a result, the city became a stimulating center of both Polish and Jewish culture, especially after Poland became a free nation again at the end of World War I, after it had been eliminated for 138 years.

View of the city of Lwów from the High Castle Park at sunset

JINGLE BELLS

The day my mother went into labor, Lwów was covered by a thick layer of snow. My father was out hunting when she had her first contractions. By the time he returned home, it was high time to rush her to the hospital. Mother was to be brought to the Salus clinic, a private hospital where my family always went.

Father hired a sleigh. We couldn't take our car, because it didn't have a heater and was locked up in the garage during the winter months. And besides, it was much safer this way with all the excitement.

So, my last trip in my mother's womb took place on a horse-drawn sleigh.

A STAY-AT-HOME

In the delivery room, my mother pushed as hard as she could, but I wouldn't budge. It seemed that I wasn't ready to enter this world yet. I had grown too attached to what I knew as my home and refused to leave it.

OUT OF THE OVEN

I was so stubborn that they had to use high forceps to pull me out. Resisting at that too, the doctor had to apply force. Thus, I looked pretty damaged when I finally saw the light of day.

The moment my dear brother Wacek saw me, he shrugged his shoulders and flatly stated that "our baby did not turn out right".

Wacek, now with a baby Brother

CHRISTMAS GIFT

Five or six days later, around Christmas, our faithful cook Hania came to the hospital to pick me up and bring me home. This time I traveled by taxi.

From the moment Hania laid eyes on me, I was her darling. She proudly carried me into our five-room apartment home on the second floor of our four-storey house. This is how I moved into my "new home" located on Saint Marek Street number 2.

Lwów, Saint Marek Street 2

POZNAŃ COUNTRY EXHIBITION

I was breast-fed for one and a half years, up until the day Father wanted to take Mother to the country exhibition in Poznań. On that day he sat down beside me and, without mincing words, instructed me to forget my "old" mother.

I obeyed. On that day, I stopped drinking my mother's milk and switched voluntarily to the baby bottle. With that problem solved, my parents got into the car and drove off to the exhibition.

HANIA

We had a cook, housekeeper, chauffeur, governess and a laundress who worked for us, but Hania was the undisputable boss amongst our domestic staff. She was a faithful soul with a big heart, and she loyally stayed with us until the day we had to leave Lwów.

LAUNDRY DAY

The laundress came once a month. On that particular day, Hania was usually in a bad mood; she had to help the laundress carry the dirty laundry down to the basement and into the washing room, watch that she did her job properly, and then drag the wet clothes up to the attic where she hung them up to dry.

On those days, Hania didn't cook us dinner. Instead, we would either eat at Babcia's, our maternal grandmother who lived below us, or dine in the Pomorzanka restaurant on Akademicka Street.

The next day, things would return to normal. Hania didn't mind the last stage of the laundry process, which was to take the freshly washed clothes down the street to get them pressed. This was where she met up with her friends and picked up the latest gossip.

KITCHEN CHILD

Wacek often made fun of me for hanging around Hania. He called me a "kitchen child", especially when he wanted to start a fight with me and I would flee into the kitchen and hide behind Hania.

I didn't care that he called me that, because I could always be sure that Hania would defend me just like a lioness defends her cubs.

The Szybalski Boys

I think he was jealous that Hania was always spoiling me with sweets and other delicious delicacies. She was a great cook and could whip up a wonderful dish out of nothing.

FOUNDLING

As I mentioned before, I wasn't born a pretty baby. On the day of my birth, a beautiful little girl was born to the Hulimka family in the Salus clinic. They were wealthy landowners. Since my mother had been hoping her second child would be a girl, Wacek maliciously claimed that her wish had been granted, but that the Hulimka family had managed to snatch their daughter from her and gave me to Mother in return. Every so often, he'd tease me by calling me a Hulimka. If he really wanted to get me angry, he'd call me a Salus foundling.

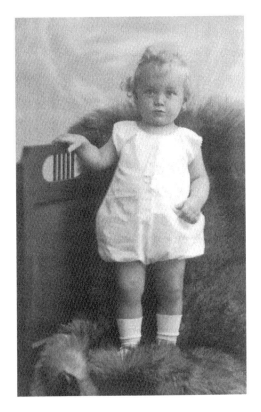

"Foundling? I'm not a foundling!"

Being called a foundling was even more painful; it evoked the feeling of not being wanted.

This teasing and name-calling terribly hurt me, and I would respond accordingly – and hit him as fiercely as I could. Of course, Wacek would not let an attack go unchallenged. As soon as he set after me, I would run and seek protection from Hania.

NOTHING BUT A TEASE

It took me a few years until I finally understood that his foundling story was total nonsense.

Moreover, I doubt that such accidents were possible in the renowned Salus clinic which had very good service and where only very few children were born.

INSTANT REPLAY

Nevertheless, it was a never-ending story that my brother loved to tease me with. It tickled him to watch how one word would always unleash the same chain reaction: He'd call me a Hulimka, I'd start to cry or scream and within seconds Hania would come running out of the kitchen, her hands in the air ready to save me.

Hania was short, but very strong and even more determined to rescue me from my pugnacious bigger brother. Surprisingly, she could wrestle him to the floor and even pin him on his back.

PA!

Ever since I can remember, I have had a soft spot for hats and caps. I was so infatuated by these accessories that I decided to make up my own word for them. It was customary in those days to tip or take off your hat when greeting others. From that ritual, I created the word "pacia" derived from the expression "pa!" with means "Hello" or "Good-bye" in colloquial Polish.

One day, during our summer vacation in Brzuchowice, my parents suddenly realized that I had disappeared. I was only two years old, so my family and their friends immediately set out into the surrounding woods to find me. It didn't take long until someone discovered me – walking stark naked through the forest. That is, almost naked. I proudly donned Father's hat that I had snatched from him while he was taking an afternoon nap on the veranda.

THE GORGONOWA STORY

During that same summer, the murder of a girl named Elżbieta Zarembianka was still the talk of the town, although it had occurred the previous winter. A woman named Emilia Margerita Gorgonowa was accused of killing the sixteen-year-old daughter of a successful architect.

The house we rented for the summer was not far from the crime scene. Even though I was too small to understand the murder case, I got it in my head that I would be the next victim. I was afraid to fall asleep and tried to stay awake each night.

Many of the mysteries and the questions I still had about the case finally cleared up when the movie "The Gorgonowa File" came out in 1977. I greatly appreciated the film, all the more for its pictures of Lwów and a car with an old Lwowian license plate. It was just like the ones our cars had, and will always stay ingrained in my memory.

DRIVE MY CAR

My father loved cars. Wacek still owns Father's cigarette box with the emblem of the Polish Automobile Club as well as miniature logos of the cars produced back then. It's quite interesting to note that although most of the cars are no longer produced, their logos are periodically updated.

My father and one of his beloved cars

As far as I remember, Father was president of the local automobile club and one of the organizers of the Grand Prix car races in Lwów for a period of time. Thanks to his position, we always had the best seats in the honorary stands along the major roadway, Pełczyńska Street. I remember how he inspected the hay bales that were set up on the dangerous curves before each race.

Father, a car enthusiast through and through

During that time, mostly Hans Stuck and Rudolf Caraciolla in their Alfa-Romeo, Austro-Daimler or Mercedes won the races. My favorite car was the Bugatti 2.3 liter, in which Polish driver Janek Ripper made second place.

GONE WITH THE WIND

My father changed his cars every so often. His first prized possession was a Brenabor that had acetylene headlights. That was before I was born; I have never been able to actually see one in real life.

Father went through various models of Fiat, Essex and Hudson. I fondly remember a Studebaker I liked to call "stary bakier" which means "old slanted cap".

He also owned a Tatra convertible whose top he unfortunately never opened lest it could blow away his hat and mess up his "loan" as mother jokingly called his painstakingly crafted hairstyle.

Father's Studebaker

UNCLE ZYGMUNT

Once on Easter, my Godfather, Father's brother Zygmunt, visited us. He was a tall and good-looking bachelor. He presented his best side in his "kontusz", a traditional and elegant Polish nobleman's suit in the 15th-19th centuries.

Uncle Zygmunt in his kontusz

CURIOSITY KILLED THE HAT

Uncle Zygmunt brought me a wonderful fireman's helmet as a gift. Unfortunately, it didn't last very long as I immediately took it apart, just like I did with all my other toys. I was obsessed with finding out how things were constructed or what mechanisms lay beneath the outer layer.

My Godfather had an unusual, deep voice. And it was loud. So loud, he didn't have to use the phone to call his coachmen, who lived on the border of his estate down by the edge of the forest.

My brother always claimed that I inherited Uncle Zygmunt's voice...

LEARNING BY DOING

Uncle slept in the salon which was also used as a guest room. I visited him once in the morning and found him sitting upright in bed smoking. I curiously asked him how the cigarette tasted. He handed it to me and told me to find out for myself.

I had barely inhaled when I started to cough. As soon as I was able to breathe normally again, I reproachfully asked him how he could give a child such terrible thing. But he just smiled, took the cigarette back and silently took another drag.

My family found this pedagogical tactic quite amusing. Even though I tried several times since, I never learned to like cigarettes. Looking back, that was my good luck.

STREET CARS

Uncle Zygmunt lived on an estate in the countryside and was accustomed to the peaceful sounds of Mother Nature. He didn't like the city and couldn't understand how we could sleep with the street cars he claimed were constantly either rolling "over the ceiling" or "over our roof".

KIDNEY STONES

I was three years old when Mother developed serious health problems. She visited various doctors, underwent the most sophisticated tests they offered at the time to find out what was wrong with her. Finally, one of the physicians found that her pains were caused by kidney stones.

COOL REACTION

In those days, the removal of kidney stones was a serious proposition and the operation potentially fatal. Understanding the gravity of the doctor's diagnosis, Mother made the best of her situation and decided to book a cruise before surrendering herself to the scalpel.

SHIP AHOY!

She went to the travel agency and selected the "In Search of the African Sun" cruise on board the S/S Polonia. Her trip began in Gdynia and led through Kiel and the English Channel, along the Atlantic coast via Gibraltar to the Mediterranean Sea.

She visited Portugal, Spain, Morocco and Tangiers among other ports. We were thrilled with the many souvenirs and gifts she brought back for us. And Mother was very pleased with herself as well, since she hadn't paid any custom duties for any of these purchases.

Mother in Seville

DR. MEHRER

I don't remember exactly how long she waited upon her return to have the operation in the Salus clinic, but finally came that day when she decided she was ready to face her fate.

Dr. Mehrer, the best urologist in Lwów, performed the operation. While Mother was under anesthesia, he discovered that one of her kidneys was damaged to the point that it endangered Mother's life and was forced to remove it. Oddly enough, he felt so bad about it that he didn't tell her when she awoke as not to worry her. Years passed until she finally learned that she now only had one kidney.

In spite of her initial shock and irritation over his behavior, Mother remained a devoted admirer of Dr. Mehrer and his loyal patient until the day in 1942 when he was taken to the Ghetto of Lwów during the German occupation. We lost all track of him. Most likely he was murdered there.

KIDDIE MOUNTAIN

Already since my early childhood, it was not hard to tell that I was neither an athletic type, nor did I have the stuff to become a ski pro. Therefore, I was completely content with skiing down the hills in Lwów's Stryjski Park, otherwise called Kiddie Mountain.

WRONG DECISION

One day, on my way home from a full day of skiing, I was too lazy to take off my skis and decided to slide down the inclined path by the park's pond instead. I found out too late, there was ice on the road. I lost my balance and fell. My bad luck was that the skis – in those days made of solid wood with child-proof guards – were too heavy to be opened by the weight of a child. In addition, my left leg got caught by one of the posts lining the park's path. As I fell, the post held back my leg. Pain shot through my body and I screamed.

HOME SERVICE

One of the passers-by brought me home on his sleigh. My nanny Fila opened the door and literally panicked. My mother immediately called Dr. Mehrer.

Even though Dr. Mehrer was a urologist, he came right away and correctly diagnosed that my leg was broken. He called for Dr. Gruca, an orthopedic surgeon, and ordered an X-ray. Please bear in mind that this all occurred in 1933, when technical standards were nowhere near what they are today. In those days, an X-ray machine was a really big deal. The machine was the size of a cabinet and had to be transported by two strong men.

My Grandma, Babcia, broke her left hip in 1916 and she was x-rayed at home, too.

CUSTOM-MADE TRACTION

The X-ray revealed that I had a spiral fracture and had broken my leg in three places. Dr. Gruca applied a traction made out of the wooden handle of a broomstick and connected it to the upper corner of my child-sized bed. Then, he wrapped tape around my leg and attached a wooden ruler at the tip of my bed which he connected to a weight made with a sand-filled pillowcase. There I had my own hand-crafted traction device – 100% custom-made.

DR. GRUCA

Dr. Gruca didn't have any patience for a spoiled Mama's baby like me. In contrast to Dr. Mehrer, he treated me very harshly. And I didn't like that at all.

I began to associate his attitude, the traction and his visits with pain. I only had to hear his footsteps approaching, and I'd start to scream and cry. Needless to say, that was very unpleasant for everyone in the house.

PLASTER OF PARIS PHOBIA

After having my leg in traction for six weeks, Dr. Gruca came to put my leg in a cast that I was to bear for another six weeks.

When my leg was wrapped in plaster, I panicked, fearing Dr. Gruca would not only plaster my leg but also my entire pelvis, and I would not be able to pee. It was at this moment he revealed to me that he did have a heart when he taught me how to pee while in the cast, and assured me that I'd soon be back to normal.

UNNERVING HEALING PROCESS

The cast brought about a new and very annoying problem – unbearable itching. The fact that I couldn't scratch my leg drove me "up the wall". It was not surprising that I had difficulties sleeping, and I often cried at night. As a result, Fila was moved into my room and had to sleep next to me.

Wacek recounts how I whined and complained and constantly said: "Es kitzelt, es kitzelt" (it tickles, it tickles) to make sure Fila, who was German, understood me.

When the cast was finally removed, my leg was one centimeter longer than before. But at least I didn't limp anymore. I went to rehab where I got baths and massages and had to do exercises.

DELUXE TREATMENT

A few years later, Father told me that the convalescence of my leg cost as much as a new car. In those days, people of better standing didn't make use of the services offered by health insurance. Actually, I don't know if we even had a health insurance.

House visits were a luxury, but my parents deemed them necessary and besides, Dr. Gruca was the best orthopedist in Lwów. After the war, he became the most famous orthopedist in Poland and his expertise was sought after throughout Europe.

TRUSKAWIEC

To compensate for the removal of one kidney, Mother spent three weeks every year in Truskawiec until the outbreak of the war. Truskawiec is a renowned spa in the Carpathian Mountains that specializes in urinary ailments. Thanks to the treatments, she lived to the age of 85.

Me, Mother and Wacek

Mother and me in Truskawiec

LOW SODIUM

Mother never had any problems with only one kidney. She just had to watch her diet, avoid sorrel and spinach and reduce her salt intake. That's why our meals at home were always low in sodium.

That is something that has stuck with me through the present. My brother, on the other hand went the other way in that respect. He always grabs the salt shaker, even before he has tasted the food.

TRAVELLING WITH BABCIA

In 1933, when I was five years old, I spent my summer vacation with Babcia, Mother's mother. We went to Skole in the eastern Carpathians and were accompanied by her lady's companion, as personal assistants were called in those days.

Babcia ordered a horse carriage to bring us to the train station.

Babcia in 1933

She preferred coaches over taxis, because she had difficulties getting in and out of a car.

In order to be sure he'd get the job, a day before departure, the coachman made a one-zloty deposit, as it was custom then. The coachman came even earlier than expected, because he was afraid he might not get his deposit back. He loaded our luggage into the wagon and drove us to the station.

WHITE GLOVES

Even though the train ride to Skole didn't last long, Babcia insisted that I wear white gloves. That way, in case I got hungry and needed to eat, my hands would be clean.

Our picnic basket contained the usual victuals – hard-boiled eggs with salt, tomatoes with salt, and either a banana or an orange.

SKOLE

When we arrived at Skole station, a carriage sent by our hosts, the Agopsowicz family was already waiting for us. The coachman drove us to their guest house, "Skolanka".

We got a nice room on the second floor in the front of the building. It had a balcony and was close to the common bathroom.

CREEPY FALLERS

We soon found out that the nice looking bush under the balcony was inhabited by gross-looking green caterpillars. They liked to crawl up the wall into our room and sometimes they would even drop from the ceiling onto our beds. They utterly disgusted me. My horrified screams would echo into the other guest rooms every time they invaded my space.

Enjoying the summer in Skole.

When we went out, we either walked with the help of Babcia's lady's companion or rode around by carriage. Babcia had problems walking – she had broken her hip during World War I and since then couldn't move about without her elegantly crafted black ebony cane.

Bacia and me in Skole

SURPRISE VISIT

One day my father stopped by for a visit and took us for a ride around town. I had completely forgotten about this event, until a few years ago. Monika, the granddaughter of the Skolanka proprietors, sent me a photograph documenting his visit.

The first thing I noticed on the photo was our car parked in the front of the guest house; it took me a second look until I recognized that the man talking to the owners was indeed Father.

JEWISH FUNERALS

Skole was a small but popular summer resort with a majority of Jewish inhabitants and vacationers. The Agopsowicz were Polish-Armenian and the only non-Jewish inn proprietors in Skole.

I'll never forget the sound of Jewish funerals in Skole. Our guesthouse was located on the way to the kirkut, the Jewish cemetery. Every time someone died, a group of wailing women would slowly pass under our balcony. It was haunting and made me feel very uneasy.

At the end of the vacation, my Mother came to pick me up and take me home.

LESZEK

The following fall, I started kindergarten, which was managed by the nuns of Notre Dame. My friend and cousin Leszek went there as well.

I don't remember too much about that, I just know that the nuns were very kind to us and we played a lot, that is, if Leszek wasn't in a bad mood for one reason or another. In that case, I'd have to wait until he managed to snap out of his sulking mood.

There was a saying that, "He who sulks, should tie his nose to a tree and carry it around with him until he snaps out of his moodiness".

Maybe Leszek should've tried out that method...

My cousin Leszek

BAWARKA BACKWARDS

Leszek might have been difficult but for his age, he surely was one of a kind. He came to my place very often. After playing, we'd have tea with milk, which was called bawarka. Older children drank tea without milk, but we were not even near that stage yet.

Tea was served either with a piece of cake or a sandwich. It was customary to take a bite of the sandwich and rinse it down with tea. Leszek made a point of doing it the other way around: He demonstratively drank his bawarka first, and then ate his sandwich. During this ritual, he'd flatly ignore the uproar he evoked in our nanny or my mother. Leszek wasn't a bad boy; it was just that during the tea and cake ceremony, he liked to be a little rebel.

Looking back at my childhood, I'd like to say a few words about the governesses who crossed the lives of me and my brother.

BRINGING UP BABY – NANNY NUMBER ONE

First, there was Ziunia. She was my first nanny and came right after I was born. I don't remember her, for I was too small. But I have heard many stories about her. There were, in fact, so many diverse tales in the air, that I will refrain from commenting.

All I know is that she was short and unattractive, but supposedly very interested in sex.

But back then, I was a bit young to understand anything about that matter.

Me in Stryjski Park, taken by Aunt Zosia, Leszek's mother

THE GERMAN ANGLE

After Ziunia, Mother decided that our nannies should be well grounded in German, so that we'd learn how to speak the language fluently.

With that new criterion in mind, she contacted a Lutheran pastor. He recommended taking in daughters of German settlers. There were many of them in the nearby Stryj area and in the province of Wołyn. They had been brought into the area to teach Ukrainian peasants how to manage their farms.

FILA

The first German nanny was Fila. She was bright and I liked her a lot. I think that we learned as much German from her as she learned Polish from us. Unfortunately, she only stayed with us for a few years. She slipped out of our lives when she got married.

Her parents grew watermelons and pumpkins and even though she no longer worked for us, she promised to bring me pumpkin seeds after the harvest. But for some reason she didn't keep her word and I never saw her again.

SMIGUS DYNGUS

I am sure Fila wasn't punishing me because of what my brother and I did to her on Easter Monday in 1934, if I remember correctly.

Easter Monday is the day we traditionally celebrate Smigus Dyngus, a humorous Polish custom with which young people douse others with water – or spray their victims with cologne.

Knowing that our father was strictly off limits on this day, because he abhorred anything that would ruin his carefully crafted hairstyle, Wacek and I sought out unsuspecting Fila. Easter Monday was her day off, so she had spent hours the evening before working her hair with a curling iron.

Our water attack came as a total surprise. Fila was so stunned, she began to cry. She immediately ran in the bathroom to wet and redo her hairdo, trying to save what was left of it, but she unfortunately only partially succeeded.

We felt very guilty and learned a good lesson: Think before you act.

ELZA

With Fila's place then vacant, the pastor sent a girl called Elza. I didn't like her. Mother didn't either, so she was let go very soon. Years later, I learned that she was arrested and incarcerated for communist activities. So even if I was just a small boy, it seems my gut feeling served me well.

EMMA

Our last nanny was Emma Vonau. I'll never forget her family name. She lived on Wronowska (Crow) Street and was previously the lady's companion of a friend of my grandmother's. Wacek and I jumbled the words and called her "Emma the Crow from Vonau Street".

Emma was not only pretty, but also had her own apartment and was very independent. That's why she only spent the daytime with us.

THE BIRDS AND THE BEES

I loved going for walks with Emma, because she was so entertaining and knew so many things about the birds and trees and the change of seasons. We often went through Stryjski Park which was much more interesting than the botanical garden.

Emma's beauty also affected my brother. He fell in love with her and a romance ensued. Thanks to her, Wacek not only learned German, but also new and exciting things about life. I can imagine that today such a love affair with an adolescent would not end as happily as theirs did. Emma left us when I entered first grade.

The next person Mother hired was Mila who was a nanny and maid all in one.

Mila and me in Stryjski Park

THE BOTANICAL GARDEN

The botanical garden was a large park surrounded by a huge brick wall. It was the favorite hangout among the youngsters of the university staff.

I personally found it quite boring there, but at least it was quiet. There were many more attractions in Stryjski Park and it was open to everyone.

HAVEN OF THE SCIENCES

Bordering on the garden were two buildings of Lwów's old university. One of them belonged to the chemistry department where Mother once studied crystallography. That building is located right across from my grandparent's house on Długosza Street, named after a Polish historian of the Middle Ages, Jan Długosz.

In order to enter the botanical garden, you had to present proper identification to the guard in front of the main entrance. Luckily, Wacek and I had passes from Professor Czekanowski, so we could enter the garden which was normally only accessible to university staff and students.

PROFESSOR RUDOLF WEIGL

On the other side of the botanical garden, Professor Dr. Rudolf Weigl worked. Here, in the rooms of the university's biology department, he invented the first effective vaccine against typhus fever.

Professor Weigl saved thousands of people, as well as my family during World War II, by giving us work under the Soviet and later German occupation in what then became known as the Typhus Institute.

WARSAW

After I graduated from kindergarten, Mother, Wacek and I spent the summer vacationing by the Baltic Sea. We took the night train to Warsaw and spent the following day there. The Polish capital was half way to our destination and the majority of our relatives as well as many friends of our parents lived there.

AUNT JANKA

We visited "Aunt" Janka, one of Mother's very good friends. She lived in a gorgeous villa in the Żoliborz district of Warsaw. What I remember about that visit was that her house was filled with film production equipment. I found it highly fascinating to have movie equipment in one's home, but the story behind it was quite a sad one.

Her husband-to-be had been a partner of Studio Feniks, a film company that produced many Polish movies. Tragically, he died during an operation, just before they were to get married and left his bereaved fiancée with his company's inventory.

BEACH DREAMS

In the evening, we left for Gdynia which we reached the following morning. We rented a room in the Saint Andrzej Bobola Villa situated at the bottom of Kamienna Góra, directly on the shore. Every day, we walked to the beach dressed in our swimming attire and sandals, and armed with beach towels and blankets in search of the perfect spot to relax and play. Ever since that vacation, I've wanted to live near the beach.

Little did I know that my wishes would be answered; a decade later my dream came true when I spent twelve years after the war in the seaside resort of Sopot and lived right near the beach. Fifty years later in the U.S., I moved to the water front when I retired and bought a house lying directly on a canal leading to the Gulf of Mexico.

FIREWORKS GALORE

During our stay in Gdynia, a highly publicized convention, "Poles Living Abroad", took place. I immensely enjoyed watching the boats and ships parade before our house. The highlight of the event was a big fireworks display on the water. That evening my mother and brother put me to bed and went to the beach front to watch the celebration.

The noise of the rockets woke me up and frightened me so much that I ran to the owner of the guesthouse for protection. Wacek made fun of me when he came home and heard how scared I'd been by fireworks.

OUT TO SEA

Aunt Kazia's husband was the director of the Sea and Colonial League. Its chairman was General Orlicz Dreszer, a hospitable and very generous man who lent us one of his motor boats, so we could go for rides and visit the Hel peninsula and Pierwoszyno.

My uncle Stas had an estate and a summer resort in Pierwoszyno. Aunt Jagoda, Uncle Dziunio and their daughter Renia spent their summers there. This was very practical, since this way we could visit two families at once.

Our eagerness to visit places by boat briefly came to a halt when the boat engine wouldn't start when we were ready and had to return home in the evening. We searched for alternative ways to get back home over land which would have been quite difficult. Luckily, the boatman managed to get the engine running again, so we were able to return home.

A CHILD'S PERSPECTIVE

One of the best things I remember about this vacation was Walt Disney's "Three Little Pigs" feature I saw at the movies. Another highlight that summer was my discovery of Gdynia's famous waffle rolls. They were a heavenly dream filled with cream. All the more so, as you couldn't buy this delicacy in Lwów. Back in those days, dieting was unheard of, so I really indulged in them.

UNCLE BRONEK AND AUNT CESIA

Upon our way home to Lwów, we made another stopover in Warsaw, this time to visit family. That is where I met my father's oldest brother, Uncle Bronek, his wife, Aunt Cesia and their two daughters, Wanda and Marysia, who everybody called Lalunia.

Aunt Cesia was very hospitable and really made sure you got enough to eat. She would give you second helpings even before you finished your first. The only way out of this situation was to eat very slowly.

Uncle Bronek and Aunt Cesia

FATAL ATTRACTION

Even though I am jumping ahead in time and fast tracking into World War II now, I feel compelled to mention the sad stories of these two cousins Wanda and Lalunia at this point.

They were later married to Polish Army officers. During the ensuing war, Wanda's husband was killed in Katyń by the Soviets, while Lalunia's husband was captured by the Germans.

At first he thought he was lucky when he managed to escape from the POW camp, but upon his return he found out that Lalunia was betraying him with another Polish officer.

If fate hit him a heavy blow, it was nothing compared to what happened to his unfaithful wife.

Little did Lalunia foresee that her attraction to a man who spied for the British would cost her her life.

LALUNIA AND MOABIT

One day Gestapo agents quietly entered her lover's apartment. They arrested him and turned his home into a kocioł, which means big pot in Polish. The kocioł was a common and efficient method Germans used to catch conspirators: Just like a spider ready for its prey, the agents patiently waited for people connected with the spy to knock on the door.

When they had arrested all the people they wanted, they would load the culprits onto a truck and take them to the Gestapo's headquarters on Aleja Szucha.

One of the unfortunate visitors was Lalunia. They knew that she was his lover and accused her of complicity. Uncle Bronek spent a fortune trying to buy his daughter's freedom. His money was taken, but his pleas were ignored.

Lalunia was brought to Moabit prison in Berlin and beheaded with an axe – as was the German custom for executing spies.

GERMAN ANSWER TO TRAITORS

The same thing happened to Renate von Natzmer, the woman who helped Polish spy, Jerzy Sosnowski, before World War II. Curiously, whereas she was beheaded, he survived and was exchanged for a German spy instead.

Even though his life was spared, he was later accused in Poland of being a double agent. Incidentally, he was a childhood friend of my Mother and Uncle Dziunio.

3. (1934–36) SAINT JOSEF PRIMARY SCHOOL

FIRST GRADE

Upon our return to Lwów, I began my school career. Saint Josef Primary School was a private school located on 9 Lelewela Street and was managed by a fraternity of the John de LaSalle order.

Mr. Gryksztas was my principal teacher, and Brother Bonawentura taught us religion. I met the latter 55 years later in Częstochowa and showed him my first grade class picture. He claimed he actually remembered me!

MY CLASSMATES

I remember a few class mates from first grade.

- Rysio Grundman, whose brother was my brother's classmate. He became a close friend of mine, but since his story is more detailed I will get back to him later.

- Stas Brunarski, son of the contractor of Lwów's New Technical University building, was drafted in 1946 to serve in the Polish Army. His unit was sent to fight the remnant of the Ukrainian Liberation Army (UPA). The UPA had escaped from the Soviet-annexed territory of eastern Poland and went on to fight against the Soviets and Poles on the new Polish eastern border. I saw him again after he returned from the service. Unfortunately, we later lost contact until a few years ago when I learned that he had died.

- Dziubek. I don't remember his full name. For years, we sat together on the same bench – I was there because I always talked too much in class. He was the son of an insurance executive; very polite, well-mannered and not too talkative. I remember that his sandwiches always had the bread crust cut off, because he didn't like to chew. Under Soviet occupation, he was deported to Kazakhstan and that's where I lost contact with him.

- Janusz Krysa, son of a judge and my friend. He tragically succumbed to the same fate as Dziubek.

- Adaś Chlipalski, son of a state prosecutor, who was also deported to Kazakhstan, but survived. I found him a few years ago through the Polish Lwów Discussion Group over the Internet. He now lives in Montreal and we are still in touch.

- Jurek Wilimowski, called Wiluś, the only classmate I've had contact with all this time and still do today. He is retired and lives in Wrocław. The last time we met was in 1991, during the reunion of the Saint Josef School in Częstochowa.

- Roman Węgrzyn and a kid called Sowiński and finally, a boy called Szczurowski who never even tried to be a good student. His father worked for Lwów's streetcar company which was reason enough to be made fun of.

ANGEL FACE

Writing, math and religion classes didn't leave any noteworthy memories behind. But I will never forget that because I was blond and my mother had always wanted a daughter, she decided I should have a pageboy style haircut which brought out my "angelic" features. That predestined me to play the role of the angel during the St. Nicolas performance on December 6th, where I had to pass out gifts to the children.

I involuntarily continued my angelic career at the subsequent Christmas school performance. Mother especially had a satin dress tailored for me. Wacek happily offered to attach angel wings to my costume.

To top things off, I wore a gold headband with a star on my head. Someday, I will find the photo that documented this "unforgettable" moment.

WITHOUT SUPERVISION

Since Leszek went to a public school which was part of the pedagogic junior college, we only met after school to "socialize". We got closer again when his father died shortly after, and his mother moved into an apartment two blocks away from us.

Thanks to that, we could meet when I visited him without having Mila or Mother watch over us. They had a corner room with a huge balcony where we could play without supervision, as his mother was at work.

Leszek and I ice-skated a lot during the winter months and we often fell on our "private body parts", as one would elegantly call the behind in those days.

After Leszek broke his arm, I would either skate alone or in the company of Mother or Mila. I remember I often had ice-cold feet and Mila would always rub them warm for me. Sometimes we went to Stryjski Park to sleigh instead; even more so after I broke my leg and I had to take a break from skiing.

MARSHAŁ PIŁSUDSKI

In the beginning of May 1935, our national leader Marshał Piłsudski died. He was the first chief of state (1918–22) of the newly independent Poland. After leading a coup d'état in 1926, he rejected an offer of the presidency, but remained politically influential while serving as minister of defense until his death.

All the newspapers carried pictures of his funeral on the front page. Our Sunday newspaper, the Cracow Courier, brought out a Piłsudski special, as did the weekly PAT Newsreels. The entire Polish nation mourned Piłsudski's death. Even in the schools, projects dedicated to his life and death were initiated.

Marshał Piłsudski

BREAK TIME

Before I noticed, my first year at school came to an end. I received good grades and fulfilled my parent's expectations. So now I was ready for a summer vacation. My brother went to Spała, to attend a Boy Scout jamboree while I spent the holidays with my parents.

We traveled to Zaleszczyki. It is the most southern town in Poland, a place where grapes, watermelons and corn grow. I loved corn then and I still love it today.

ROMANIA

In order to get to Zaleszczyki, you had to travel through Romania. When we crossed the border, Romanian soldiers got onto the outside steps of the train wagons. It was shocking to see how pathetic and squalid they looked, especially in comparison to the Polish soldiers that I admired for their elegant appearance.

I was told that Romania was a poor country that couldn't afford to provide nice uniforms for its soldiers. But on the other hand, their officers were dressed very well and even wore corsets under their uniform, probably to make a better figure.

ZALESZCZYKI

Our holiday destination was situated on the left bank of the Dniestr River, which surrounds the town on three sides and forms the border between Poland and Romania.

In contrast to the sad-looking Romanian river bank, the Polish side was lined with remarkably elegant summer residences, beaches and guesthouses, hotels and restaurants with well-tended recreation areas. But the farther you got from the beach, the more humble the houses were.

Mother and me in Zaleszczyki

BEACH ATTIRE

We stayed in a guesthouse which was popular among the intelligencia of Lwów. We had a room with a balcony and a view of the river. When I think of that summer, I always see my father in his funny-looking bathing suit that he must have bought a very long time before when we was vacationing on the French Riviera. My mother always wore her big sun hat to protect herself from the sun.

My parents were acquainted with a family that owned a kayak called "My Boy". Not knowing English then, I didn't grasp the meaning of the name. Mother and Father often went on excursions in the kayak. Sometimes they also took me along. Since that summer I've dreamt of owning such a kayak.

DASHING DANCER

After I was put to bed, my parents regularly went out dancing. One evening, Father was elected the most elegant man, and he received the title, "Best Dressed Man" as well. Thanks to this, I became popular among the children in our guesthouse.

SAND MOTORBOAT

That summer, we had non-stop great weather and a lot of sunshine. Unfortunately, the lack of rain lowered the water level of the Dniestr to such an extent, that boat cruises were no longer possible. The only way you could travel on water was by motorboat. I remember "building" such a motorboat out of sand, with which I pretended to be riding down the Dniestr.

Vacation with parents in Zaleszczyki, 1935

CONTENT WITH LITTLE

I guess we stayed as long in Zaleszczyki as Wacek was in Spała. Upon our return to Lwów, we met up with him. He, Mother and I continued on to Skole to visit Babcia.

I had already been to Skole before, but in comparison to my brother and mother, I was much more active. I went swimming a lot. The water level was low here too, but it was enough for me to play.

Babcia and me in Skole

YIDDISH ENTERTAINMENT

My fun and water games made me the center of attraction for the Hasidic Jews whose leader Cadyk and his entourage sunbathed on the rocks. They wore paper hats made of Yiddish newspapers to protect their heads from the sun and joked loudly about my splashing around.

Vacation in Skole

We also frequented a local park which is where we met Cadyk. He and his entourage loved to eat onion cake. I wanted to try it, but for some reason my mother refused to buy me some.

Once, I wandered off to the five o'clock dance, which everybody just called "the Five". My mother and brother loved to go dancing at this time. Wacek was and still is a big dancing devotee, even at his advanced age.

We also made excursions to Ławoczne by train. Ławoczne was a border town to Carpathian Ruthenia which then was a part of Czechoslovakia. Later, just before the outbreak of the war, it was taken in by Hungary when Poland had a common border with Hungary. We didn't cross to the other side since the political relations with our neighbors weren't good then and in addition, Mother said there was "nothing interesting to see".

Me, Mother and Wacek in Skole

SECOND GRADE

After summer break, I began second grade. I was seven years old, but not much happened.

I remember that Szabajko, with whom I horsed around a lot, was no longer in my class. Rumor had it that his mother was very interested in the young and good-looking Mr. Gryksztas, who no longer taught at our school and that she had followed him.

Not always an angel... (Taken during my first communion)

PAINFUL BOW

Brother Grzegorz became my new class teacher. He liked to sing and play the violin, but he also used the bow to hit us when we didn't obey him immediately.

His bad temper increased, because he didn't know how to keep us under control. I remember a brief moment of comic relief on the day he tore a string on his bow and the entire class broke out with laughter.

EARN YOUR SLOPES

Right after Christmas, we went to Skole for skiing. In those days, there were no lifts, so you had to hike up the hills in order to ski down them. That sure kept you warm and occupied. The weather was sunny, but cold.

Ski Pros in Skole

MEAN TRICK

Once my brother asked me if I wanted to find out how a door-handle tastes at minus 20° Celsius. Being the naïve little boy that I was, I agreed and followed his instructions to lick the knob.

My tongue got stuck to the frozen metal. I began to scream. All the children laughed at me. I was so angry and embarrassed that I had no other choice but to end my misery by tearing my tongue off the knob. Of course, a piece of flesh remained stuck to the metal. Well, that's how my dear brother could be.

Evenings, we danced to music crackling out of the gramophone.

Winter in Skole

BACK ON THE ICE

As always, vacation went by in a flash and the return to school was impending. Once again, we performed the Christmas story and again I played the angel. The good news was that Leszek's arm was healed and finally we could enjoy afternoons ice skating again.

LUCKY TRADE-OFF

In the spring, I fell ill with scarlet fever. During my infectious phase, Wacek stayed with the Różyckis who were good friends of our grandparents. Their house was across the street from Wacek's high school, so he had only to cross the street to get to classes. The main entrance of their house had an electric gate which was quite a novelty back then.

Wacek shared the apartment of the owner's son. The son lived on the ground floor, was a bachelor and had his own balcony overlooking the street and his high school.

His parents and his aunt lived on the second floor. They had a very nice bourgeois home with parquet floors that were as shiny as a mirror, but on which you were only allowed to walk in cloth house shoes. Their balcony was connected to a hanging bridge that led to their rose garden. Marmalade made from those roses was the best I've ever tasted.

FAMOUS DAUGHTERS

The two Różycki girls roomed on the third floor. Marysia, the older sister, was a famous painter. Mother, Wacek and I had portraits done by her. Mother's and Wacek's portraits are hanging today in Wacek's home in Madison, Wisconsin, and mine adorns my living room.

The younger daughter, Kasia, was a pilot who flew airplanes on her own, something that was quite rare then. I liked her a lot, but I was unfortunately only a child. She married a pilot who broke many gliding records.

So, while I was sick at home with scarlet fever, Wacek got to live under the roof of such an interesting family. Even though my mother was at home looking after me, she'd stay in touch with my brother daily by phone.

FAMILY RITUAL

On Holy Week, we visited various churches to see the different displays of Christ's tombs. This was also the time you'd feel the first bursts of spring.

During this week, we traditionally went to the Resurrection Mass in the Armenian cathedral, located on Armenian Street in the old city. Its liturgy, though also Catholic, was different from that of the Roman Catholic Church to which we adhered.

THE ARMENIAN CONNECTION

The church had a marvelous choir, but the main reason we went there was because Leszek's grandfather's first cousin was an Armenian Catholic archbishop.

Lwów is the only city to have three Catholic archbishops:

- Roman-Catholic
- Greek Catholic
- Armenian-Catholic

QUESTION OF PRIORITIES

The topic after mass was whether one should continue fasting and not eat meat. My father claimed that you could eat meat while my Mother insisted on abstaining. Hania secretly accommodated Father's wishes by sneaking some meat onto his plate.

Me, Father and Wacek

EASTER TRADITION

It was the same story every year; I always had a sore throat and fever on Easter and had to stay in bed. I'd use the time to read more cowboy and Indian stories by Karl May who was my favorite writer at the time.

COUSIN TADZIO

In the late spring of 1936, my cousin Tadzio came to visit us. His grandfather and my grandmother were siblings. Tadzio had a very unhappy childhood, so my mother always felt obliged to look after him.

Tadzio was born in Żytomierz belonged to the part of Poland that had been occupied by the Russian empire. At the outbreak of the First World War, his father was therefore drafted as an officer into the Czar's army. His mother stayed back with her son and father-in-law who was a physician. Soon after, she died of tuberculosis.

Practically an orphan, Tadzio spent the next two years with his grandparents. During the ensuing Red Revolution, both his grandparents died of typhus. Tadzio then was taken in by his uncle's family.

BAD LUCK, PART II

Gratefully, his father returned from the war alive and sane, got a job as an administrative clerk in Wołyn, which was in the new Free Poland, and remarried. A few years later, Tadzio finally reunited with his father after his aunt smuggled him from the still Soviet Żytomierz to Poland.

Unfortunately, his fate didn't turn for the better. Tadzio's stepmother didn't like him and treated the boy badly. The fact that Tadzio wasn't easy to handle further worsened his standing. One day his father had enough and sent Tadzio off to a boarding school.

As long as Babcia Taborowska, the sister of his grandfather, was alive, things weren't so bad, because she did everything to help him. After her death, my mother took over and tried to help Tadzio however she could.

BRIEF RESPITE

I spent a lot of great moments with Tadzio. We went to the movies and for many long walks. He had a lot of patience and astonishingly, pedagogical talent. He loved to tell tales about nature. He studied agricultural science and after he graduated, took on a job as an agricultural instructor in Wołyn.

ATTENDING ONE'S OWN FUNERAL

He started to settle down and even enjoy life when he was drafted as a reserve officer a few months before World War II broke out. He fought in the September campaign against the Germans. He was caught and made a prisoner of war but fled and returned home just in time to attend his own funeral mass– unimaginable! One of his war buddies had claimed that Tadzio had died on the battle field.

TADZIO'S TRAIL

Due to Tadzio's position in the local government and being a reserve officer in the Polish Army, the Soviets were about to arrest him. Tadzio went into hiding and came to us to get help to leave the country.

NEVER-ENDING STORY

Mother gave him the address of a place near the Hungarian border. After several attempts, he finally succeeded in crossing the border. From there, he continued to Yugoslavia where he boarded a ship to Syria and from there traveled by ship to France. He arrived in France just before the German invasion in 1940. There, he joined the Polish Army in exile. His desire to fight ended when he was wounded during the invasion and then evacuated to England.

SUMMER OF 1936

As with each spring, the exciting time of walks through the park, excursions and preparation for the next summer break began. This year, the Boy Scout jamboree took my brother to Brasov-Polana in Romania.

Father and I went to the countryside to see his brother, Zygmunt. It had been a long time since I had last seen him, but as he was my Godfather, it was appropriate to visit him more regularly.

He lived in Piła near Końskie Wielkie in the Radom region in a very nice estate house. There were huge pillars framing the main entrance. It was built with an overhang so that guests arriving by horse carriage could enter the house without getting wet.

KOŃSKIE WIELKIE

To get from Lwów to Końskie Wielkie, one had to change trains twice: in Koluszki and Skarżysko-Kamienna. Końskie's train station was small and looking just like all stations along the Warsaw-Vienna railway line for which it was built.

When we arrived, my uncle was already waiting for us with his coachman in a sporty horse-drawn carriage. Uncle lacked his brother's love for cars. He preferred horses as did most of the people in the area. Zygmunt had a lot of employees on his estate. I was eight years old and this was my first visit to the countryside. Everything was so new and interesting.

A TYPICAL NOBLEMAN'S COUNTRY HOUSE

Uncle Zygmunt's house had two entrances and both led to the hallway. On one side, were the kitchen, bathroom and the servant's quarters. On the other side, a large entrance led to the living room with windows that looked out onto the drive-way and the courtyard. From the living room, you could enter Uncle's bedroom, or go to the guest rooms and the dining room.

YOGI ON THE FIRST FLOOR

There were a few other rooms on the first floor. One of them was occupied by an older man who was very much into yoga and liked to do headstands. It seemed he was also a writer of some sort. He must have eaten in the kitchen, because he never ate with us in the dining room.

THE FARM

Vegetables, sun flowers and corn were grown in the garden. On the edge of the forest, stood a stable for Uncle's four horses and a carriage house for an entire collection of different carriages.

THE STAFF

Nearby, the houses of the coachmen and the forest ranger and their families stood. One of the coachman's principal duties was to tighten the harness and prepare the horses to pick up Uncle or his guests or take them wherever they wanted to go.

Even though Uncle was modern and had a telephone, he hated to use it and preferred to shout out the assignments to his men. His voice was so loud that you could hear it all the way down to the forest.

SELF-SUFFICIENCY

In the midst of the forest, Uncle Zygmunt owned a small estate called Malachów. It consisted of an agricultural area, a fishery and a water mill in which he produced flour.

In Piła, he had a saw mill that was powered by hydraulic energy taken from the adjoining stream. When the water level was high, there was enough energy to power the entire estate, but when the water level was low, he had to use petroleum lamps and candles for light.

Zygmunt also had a large radio that was powered by a battery and charger. He liked to listen to the news – and it was very important to keep in mind not to ask "stupid" questions during its broadcast.

GO FISH!

On the other side of the garden was a pond full of fish. My father liked to fish, so we would head for the pond right after breakfast. Father caught fish using worms. I always felt nauseous when he stabbed the worms onto the hook.

I was not into fishing, but preferred to read comic books which were the latest trend.

THE TRUTH ABOUT PIKE

A forest ranger once told me to stick my finger into the mouth of a live pike. My experience until then consisted of fish filet, a de-boned piece of fish that was nicely prepared and served on a plate. I had no idea whether fish had teeth or not.

The beast bit me so hard, my finger bled. This is how I learned, the painful way, that pikes are armed with sharp teeth.

KEEPING A LOOKOUT

There were rumors that poachers were roaming the forest. For that reason, my father and uncle always carried small handguns with them.

They were both arms enthusiasts and each owned quite impressive collections. Uncle's most prized gun was a cavalry Mauser. Similar guns were popular during the Russian Revolution, as shown in the movie "Doctor Zhivago".
I didn't own a gun, but I liked pistols. The first one I possessed was when the war had ended. I had a one-month permit for it which had to be extended every month and always carried both items around with me. I had to surrender it not long after, because I was not a member of the Communist Party. Fifty years later, I got one from my wife for Christmas. In Florida, you don't need a gun permit. Today, I keep it loaded in my desk drawer.

BACK TO THE BEACH

After our visit with my Godfather, we went to Warsaw where Father and I met with Mother and Wacek. In the evening, we took the night train to Orłowo near the Baltic Sea.

NAZISM IN THE STREETS

From there, we made day excursions to the port cities Gdynia which was a brand-new city, build by Poles when they gained independence in 1918, and Gdańsk which was an independent City.

In Gdańsk, for the first time, I saw flags with a Swastika and Hitler youth in the streets. That was when I decided I no longer wanted to speak German. I wanted to distance myself as much as possible from these people.

It was in the summer of 1936.

4. (1936–39)
ENTERING THE WORLD
OF POLITICS

TOP-SECRET ENCOUNTER

As always upon our return trip home, we made a stop in Warsaw. This time, we visited Maria, called Maniusia, a good friend of Mother's. She was the second wife of Ignacy Mościcki, the third President of the Second Polish Republic. His first wife had passed away earlier. This visit really impressed me. The only condition was that we could not tell anyone about our visit. I have been true to my promise and kept this secret for decades until only recently.

BACK TO SCHOOL

Summer vacation 1936 was over and I entered third grade. This year, Brother Anzelm was our class teacher. I liked him a lot, especially since I was one of his favorite students.

COMMUNISM IN SPAIN

Ever since my mother visited Spain, I have been very interested in that country. The lack of support for the Spanish Republic by the world's leading democratic nations led to the rapid growth of communism in 1936–1939 in Spain.

I watched the rise of communism with great apprehension. For me, communism was equivalent to the devil.

COMMUNISM IN LWÓW

In my hometown, we also had problems with communist agitation. They damaged the streets, destroyed a few stores and fought with police who opposed them on their beautiful horses.

There was a famous case of a man called Kozak who was shot by a police officer. I don't remember why, but his coffin was dropped several times during the funeral march. In the end, Kozak's corpse fell out of the coffin.

I know this story only from hear-say. To top things off, this strange story happened in the center of the city, in a section of the town where Kozak neither lived nor which er ever frequented.

ON THE AIR

One day in the winter, Aunt Zosia invited me over to do a voice job at the local radio station. She wrote radio plays for

Aunt Ada who had a children's program on Lwów Radio. As Aunt Zosia was Leszek's mother, she often used him when they needed a child's voice.

It seems that I lacked my cousin's acting abilities, since I was never asked to come back...

Short career: My one-time appearance on Lwowskie Radio
Aunt Ada (second row, middle) and me (right of Ada) and Leszek (first row, right)

PROOF OF MATURITY

Let me remind you that I was eight years old and in third grade, so I was literally "almost" grown-up. My problem at that time was that my nanny still brought me to and picked me up from school. Children made fun of me because of that.

One day, I finally had enough of this. I had a talk with my parents and from then on I went to school on my own.

PSYCHIC ABILITIES

I can't remember who convinced my mother to go on a cruise to the Canary Islands. In any case, she bought a ticket and prepared herself for the trip. I didn't like the idea at all. I was afraid something would happen to her.

One week before her departure, I miraculously contracted measles. The good mother that she was, she cancelled her trip to take care of me.

Vacationing in Morszyn - on my way to becoming a Lady's man

MARCHING AND HIKING

Like all boys in those days, I was a Cub Scout. Starting in spring, we'd meet once a week to practice marching for the upcoming national holiday parade on May 3rd. After that, the school year slowly came to an end, and that meant a lot of fun-filled class excursions.

GOOD INTENTIONS

My cousin Zosia stopped by to see us on the return of one of her trips abroad. She was the daughter of my father's sister, Aunt Mania. She had studied dentistry and had just graduated. Mother liked her a lot and wanted to set her up with a nice boy. She took her along to various social meetings. Unfortunately, she didn't succeed.

As it turned out later, Zosia missed her chance since she didn't make the right pick on her own. At least she was more successful in her career. During the war, she had a dental practice in Warsaw. Almost all our relatives who lived in the area were her patients.

SUMMER PLANS

Summer arrived. My brother got to travel to Paris with a group of boys and girls from various high schools. The trip was organized by the Ministry of Education and was granted to students who had excelled with good grades. They stopped in Berlin on their way.

My mother's project for this summer was to paint our house. And I went to summer camp in Mikuliczyn, organized by my school.

HUMBLE ENVIRONMENT

This was my first summer without my parents and without the luxury I was so accustomed to. I didn't like it at all. I had to sleep on a straw mattress and my suitcase had to be stored under my bed. We were not explicitly told to wash ourselves and they only had cold water. Not only did things smell badly, the food was just inedible.

My only lifesaver was that I had cash and my savings book with me, so I could go out and buy whatever I wanted.

ENOUGH IS ENOUGH

We did a lot of hiking, and when the weather was nice, we went swimming. The river wasn't deep. It was as my father would say, "as deep as the knee of an old frog". Nevertheless, there were deep spots. Once I fell into one of them by mistake and almost drowned. Brother Grzegorz saved me, but this accident was the last straw.

I had enough. I chastised my mother and begged her to take me back home. I finally got my way and returned home – where tension was high in another way.

PAINTER POWER

In the meanwhile, my mother had got into such a serious argument with the painter, Mr. Gołębiowski, that they were forced to hire a lawyer. In the end, they finally came to a settlement, although it left both parties unsatisfied.

We had no idea that three years later, Mr. Gołębiowski would work under the Soviet occupation as a militiaman and be able to settle the matter more to his liking...

FORGET ABOUT YOUR PROBLEMS

By the time Wacek returned from Paris, the house painting issue was more or less over, or more precisely, in the hands of our lawyer.

Therefore, we were now free to go to Zaleszczyki as a family and enjoy ourselves. We spent a lot of time on the beach and in the evening, we went for walks and sang songs. Mother was most often out on her own dancing.

FOURTH GRADE

Fourth grade is when it began to get interesting. History, biology and crafts were added to our curriculum. History immediately became my passion and still is today.

BOY SCOUTS

Most importantly, now I was a Boy Scout. Wacek belonged to the first Boy Scout troupe of Lwów which was named after the Polish national hero, Tadeusz Kościuszko, which was also the first and oldest Boy Scout troupe in Poland.

They wore hats that were similar to the Boy Scouts of Australia. I greatly envied my brother for his hat.

CULTURE KICK

One day my mother decided I needed lessons in piano and French. I was quite successful in dodging the piano lessons. But that was almost impossible with French instruction. Mother hired a lady who came to our home for dinner, so that right after the meal, she could begin lessons without losing any time.

I suffered all the way until Christmas. Soon after the holidays, my French teacher fell ill and my lessons stopped. Well, at least I learned to recite 'L'Arbre de Noël'.

CLOSED SHOP

As long as I can remember, Father owned a car importing business in the most fashionable part of the city. There he imported mostly American cars and also several car brands from Czechoslovakia. In addition, he had a car repair shop with a few mechanics working for him.

In the beginning of the nineteen thirties, the Great Depression arrived in Poland, and in response, the Polish government imposed very high taxes on cars. This killed Father's business, and he had no other choice than to close it.

THE UNDERWOOD TYPEWRITER

Father liquidated most of his inventory, but brought home the few things of sentimental value, like a nice desk, which he set up in Wacek's room, and an 'Underwood' typewriter that he placed on top of a small typewriter table in the dining room. I was not allowed to use the typewriter, because he was afraid I would break it.

But temptation was stronger than discipline. Once, while my father was taking a nap, I snuck up to the desk and began to type. Unfortunately, I got caught and was in trouble for disobeying; the machine was soon sold, in spite of my wishes.

FRESH AIR

The windows were always open when my father took his daily afternoon nap. It was clearly not his choice, but Mother's decision to let in as much fresh air as possible.

Right in front of our salon window where father napped was a tree in which a family of crows had built its nest. They made a lot of noise and would wake him up every so often.

But Father knew it made no sense to argue. All things went according to Mother's will.

NEVER TEMPT A HUNTER'S TEMPER

One day Father had enough of the birds. He went to his closet and pulled out his Name's Day present – a 22-caliber Flobert gun. He calmly sat down in front of the window sill, aimed and fired. Immediately, one crow was killed and fell down. The other birds flew from the nest in a panic.

Mother never found out about Father's "hunting spree"; she just wondered why it had suddenly become so quiet outside.

GUN COLLECTION

As just mentioned, Father possessed a Flobert gun. This had been a present from the days when he was director of the "Arma" weapons manufacture. Beyond his extensive gun collection, he also owned a Browning pistol. For hunting, he used proper hunting guns, depending on what he hunted. Gun possession was very common in those days.

EQUAL RIGHTS

Mother owned a revolver. It was always loaded and hidden in her night table drawer.

There were rumors that during one summer in Brzuchowice she heard some noises and she sent a warning shot through the open window. Curiously, Wacek who was sleeping in the same room did not wake up.

Mother and me in Brzuchowice

MOVING TO WARSAW

I guess it was in the fall of 1936 when Father moved to Warsaw. He took on a job in city government. We were to follow him after Wacek graduated from high school and mother sold her apartment houses.

Neither Wacek nor I were thrilled about this plan, as we were pure-bred Leopolitans. Lwów was our home and where we wanted to stay. Besides, we didn't want to change schools and start from scratch with everything. Mother was on our side and, as a result, was in no hurry to make preparations for the move.

Me, Mother and Wacek walking on Akademicka Street, 1936

PROCRASTINATION

Father, therefore, would have to travel to Lwów to see us. He came on the holidays and some of the weekends. Mother visited him several times.

There was also the problem that we couldn't leave Babcia behind, who had just moved into our house. Mother had just split one 5-room apartment into a 2-room and a 3-room-apartment; the smaller one was for my grandmother and her lady's companion and the 3-room apartment was to be rented out.

Before a new tenant moved in, someone – we suspected our janitor Janek – entered the empty apartment and forcefully broke through the former door, now closed off by a brick wall, and stole Babcia's jewelry.

Mother and Babcia with her Lady's companion

MERRY CHRISTMAS

Christmas was wonderful that year. Father was home and brought us a lot of presents. Uncle Tadzio Arcisz from Lublin, his wife Ujcia and son Jurek also came to spend the holidays with us.

Uncle Tadzio was captain of the heavy artillery and my favorite uncle, because he was able to talk to me on my fourth-grade level. His mother owned a famous private high school in Lublin. Uncle Tadzio's wife was very affectionate and warm-hearted. She came from my mother's side of the family; my great-grandmother and her grandmother were sisters.

And then there was Mancia, who is Ujcia's third and oldest sister and my Godmother. She had a PhD in philology and taught Polish in a high school in Lublin.

Her husband Stanislaw was called Żuś and was a major in the army. His father was the president of the Veterinarian Academy in Lwów for many years.

Wacław was popular name in our family and was given in honor to our great-grandmothers' brother, Dr. Waclaw Lasocki. He was convicted for his participation in the failed Polish uprising of 1863 and sentenced to death. His death sentence was then commuted to slave labor in the salt mines of Siberia. He survived this ordeal and returned home, where he later co-founded the Nałęczów spa, which is located west of Lublin.

The charm of the town of Nałęczów was appreciated by many famous Polish writers and poets such as: Nobel prize winner Henryk Sienkiewicz, Bolesław Prus, Stefan Żeromski, and Stanisław Witkiewicz, as well as artists from abroad, and many other famous people.

Nałęczów is also the place where my parents met. My cousin Wacek Królikowski was one year older than me. He also carries our great-granduncle's name.

As I mentioned before, Christmas was quite exciting that year. When the holidays were over and everybody had left, it felt like the house had become too empty to bear.

Christmas, 1936

CINZANO

Father didn't return until Easter 1938. As always, I was sick and had to stay in bed during the holidays. In those days, the drink Cinzano was in vogue. Even I got to have a sip. After Easter dinner, the family left the house to visit relatives and friends.

My brother returned earlier that evening and asked me if I'd like to have another sip of Cinzano. I agreed, but when I drank it I realized that it wasn't Cinzano, but vinegar. That was my brother.

HITLER ON THE MOVE

This was also the time that Germany began to expand. In the beginning, Germany was officially on friendly terms with Poland. That was until Hitler annexed Sudeten and Austria.

In Poland, we believed that our army was strong enough to withstand an invasion and therefore we didn't fear the potential threat from Germany.

SUMMER IN KRYNICA

With spring came numerous Boy Scout meetings and class excursions. But instead of traveling with my classmates, I went on vacation with my parents. That year we went to Krynica, a Polish spa that is famous for its healing water. I took dancing lessons, but found out that I hadn't inherited my mother's passion or my brother's talent.

One morning, as we were walking past the Patria Hotel, we met the owners, Poland's internationally renowned opera singer Jan Kiepura and his wife Martha Eggert who was a famous Hungarian singer and actress. They were really nice and signed autographs for Father and me. I still have that postcard with their signatures.

KRYNICA. Nowy Dom Zdrojowy i Deptak

Autographed postcard of Krynica

NEWS FROM ABROAD

After our vacation in Krynica, Mother returned to Lwów whereas Father and I took the train to see Uncle Zygmunt. There, we met up with Wacek who had just returned from another summer traveling abroad. Wacek then told us about his travel experiences.

This time, he travelled through Austria to Italy where he even received an audience with the Pope. Wacek's account took on a startling turn when he told us that he saw a sign in Vienna that prohibited Jews from entering the park. It was shocking for us and we refused to believe him. We were all the more stunned when he showed us a photograph he took to prove it. The sign read "Betreten verboten für Juden".

JEWS IN LWÓW

About one quarter of the population in Lwów was Jewish. Yet they were very present in town as they owned the majority of the stores in which we shopped. In those days, there was a Jewish saying in my town: "You own the streets, we own the houses".

BACK TO THE SEA

After an eventful stay in the countryside, the three of us returned to Warsaw where Mother was awaiting us. Father returned to work while Wacek, mother and I continued to the Baltic Sea.

Mother on the beach

This time, we stayed in Lisi Jar on the top of peninsula Hel. This was the time when I wanted to be elegant and wore a marine uniform as often as I could.

Taken on Leszek's Balcony on Pelczysnka Street

FRAGILE ELEGANCE

My cousins who were staying there as well, were envious of my attire and always tried to get me dirty, but I did everything possible to stay clean and elegant.

SWASTIKA FLAGS

Upon our return, we passed through Gdynia, Orłowo and Sopot to Gdańsk. I will never forget seeing the entire city of Gdańsk bathed in Hitler's swastika flags. I was so shocked, I bought a Hitler arm band as proof to show in school.

A HAVEN OF PEACE

In Gdańsk, we met with Mother's acquaintance from Truskawiec, the director of the Polish High School in Gdańsk. He invited us to visit his school. We caught a moment of respite in what seemed to be one of the last swastika-free places. Seeing Gdańsk as it was then left a bitter after taste. It was no longer a "Free City".

After the war, when I lived in Sopot, I worked for the Regional Government that had offices very close to the former Polish high school. They were not as severely damaged as most of the city, first by the receding Germans, then by the so-called liberating Soviets who did the rest.

On our way back home, we stopped in Warsaw and spent a day with Father.

FIFTH GRADE

In the fall of 1938, I entered fifth grade. Brother Anzelm remained our class teacher. Soon after, Neville Chamberlain and Edouard Daladier signed the Munich Agreement. Hitler annexed another part of Czechoslovakia, and as some sort of compensation, Poland got Zaołdzie.

This trade caused a lot of enthusiasm and excitement in Poland. Nobody could have ever dreamt what soon would happen to us.

HIGH ALERT

In the winter of 1938, Hungary occupied autonomous Subcarpathian Ruthenia.

The visit of Polish Minister Beck to London; the British-Polish and then the French-Polish Military Alliance, guaranteeing to safeguard Poland's borders, followed by the minister's famous speech in the Polish Sejm, were the most important political topics in the Spring of 1939.

WEIRD CHANGES

After winter break, my school hired a new deputy director. He was Slovakian and hardly spoke Polish. From the start, he confronted us and our parents with changes no one liked. To make matters worse, Brother Anzelm, my class teacher since third grade was to be transferred to Częstochowa. This upset everyone since we all wanted to finish our final year in this school with him.

DEFIANT PARENTS

In response, a group of parents, including my mother got together and decided to boycott these changes by taking their children out of the school.

I was to go to the public school Leszek attended. The problem though was that classes were also taught in Ukrainian, a language that was part of the curriculum in all primary schools except for the private schools.

But I had no choice. It was decided that I was going to leave my old school by the end of the scholastic year.

ENTERING THE REAL WORLD

Meanwhile, Wacek passed his senior level exams and graduated from high school with honors. In his last summer vacation before he was going to go to officer reserve school in the fall, he attended a work camp which was compulsory for all high school graduates.

UNCLE BOGDAN

The feeling of an imminent war was in the air. Many men were drafted into military service. One of them was Uncle Bogdan Rakowski. Although he was director of a sugar industry bank, he was drafted as a veterinary reserve officer, because he had a degree in veterinary medicine.

Uncle Bogdan

LIFE-SAVING KICK

The fact that Uncle Bogdan had never practiced his civic profession as a reserve officer became evident when he got so severely kicked by a horse that it broke his arm.

The painful blow turned out to be a lucky one. Thanks to this mishap, he wasn't murdered in Katyń like so many thousands of Polish Officers. But I'll return to this subject later.

ZAKOPANE

In the summer of 1939, I went with my mother to Zakopane, Poland's answer to St. Moritz, located in the Tatra Mountains. We stayed in the Liberakówka guesthouse which is located next to the Chałubiñski monument. It was a popular inn among vacationers from Lwów.

Mother and me at Morskie Oko near Zakopane

SUPERSTITION

Being in Zakopane made Mother nervous. She was afraid a war would break out, because the last time she was in Zakopane, World War I began. Unfortunately, her superstition was closer to the truth than we wanted to believe.

Wacek's camp ended earlier than planned due to mother's connections. He joined us in Zakopane.

THE JASINSKA SISTERS

I don't know who introduced us to the Jasinska sisters, daughters of an attorney and widower. While the sisters were quite displeased that their tutor was trying to hook up with their father, they themselves were quite open to get to know the other sex. Krzysia, the older one, was pretty and soon became Wacek's girl-friend. They spent a lot of time together going for walks.

Her sister Ewa was ten years old. I liked her a lot. It was when I pushed her on the swing that she surprised me with a kiss. And a memorable summer began. Ewa was very funny – and she didn't want to go for walks with mother as a chaperone. She was very mature for her age.

Unfortunately, the last summer before World War II came to an end. We returned home. Along the way, we saw how they were already digging anti-aircraft trenches along the railroad tracks.

Ewa Jasinska a month before World War II broke out

5. (1939)
HITLER ATTACKS POLAND

THE DAY WORLD WAR II BEGAN

The first of September 1939 was a sunny day and there was no evidence that something would happen that would completely change our lives in a free Poland, and that things would never be the same again.

Right after breakfast, Wacek went with Babcia to the bank to collect her pension, while I went off in the other direction to buy school supplies. I was going to start sixth grade in a new school and I felt pretty grown up.

SCHOOL SUPPLY SHOPPING

I don't remember why I didn't go to the store which was across the street from our house, but went instead to Fredro Street, to the store owned by Jurek's father, Mr. Michotek.

Jurek was a classmate of Wacek's and later became a famous actor and singer.

I probably went to Mr. Michotek's store, because that way I could get another look at my old school along the way. Moreover, Mr. Michotek always served his clients well, not like the salesmen in the store across our street.

FIRST EXPLOSION

As I was leaving the store fully equipped for the new school year, I heard an explosion coming from the direction of Legionów Street. I thought nothing about it, assuming it was an anti-aircraft artillery test and calmly returned home.

The moment I stepped through the door I learned that the war had started and that the explosion I heard was the first German bombs falling on Lwów. We were at a loss to know what to do. We talked about covering the windows with papers strips so that in case of an explosion the glass would not burst into small pieces. We also needed to cover the windows with something dark to withhold the light at night, so that the enemy couldn't see our city from the air.

WAR PREPARATIONS

I turned on the radio in search of any information that could help us. We had a new receiver that also brought in foreign stations.

Wacek returned shortly after and told us to prepare a bomb shelter in the basement. Mother chose the empty basement that belonged to the currently vacant apartment. Hania and Janek, our janitor, went downstairs to get the place in order, take down a few pieces of furniture, and hang up a hammock.

PROVISIONS

After that, Hania checked our food reserves and went to the grocery store on the ground floor of our house to stock up on whatever she could get to keep us supplied for the next few days. She also went to the bakery to buy cookies and cakes, because we didn't know what the situation would be in the near future.

Since we expected power shortages and assumed there would be problems with supplies, Janek bought cans of kerosene from the shop that was also situated in our house and went to get coal from the store located in our former garage. Mother talked to Father by phone. He told her that if the situation didn't improve he would return to Lwów. That was the first day of the war.

DAY TWO

There were a few bombardments that went down in the outskirts of town. We learned that the situation on the Polish front was not looking good. But, in general, there was no panic.

THE RUMOR MILL CHURNS

Mr. Kiszinger was a well-known baker in Lwów. We always shopped at his bakery, because he made the best bread in town. When you bit into a fresh loaf, its crust would crunch and taste so delicious.

Mr. Kiszinger was of German descent and also had a son. Since nobody had seen the young man in a long time, word quickly spread that he was now a German pilot and was flying over Lwów and dropping bombs on us. I don't know how much truth there was in the story, but the rumors started to fly.

The local rumor mill, or the JPP News Agency (Jedna Pani Powiedziała – "A woman told me...") as we called it, kicked up. Tales passed from one person to another. The positive ones consisted mostly of wishful thinking and were unfortunately far from the truth.

DAY THREE

I don't remember much of what happened that day, except that the first wave of refugees from western Poland started to flood into Lwów.

We greeted the British and French declaration of war on Germany with great enthusiasm. Rumor had it that soon our allied friends would come to help us. They would attack the Germans from the west, which would relieve our army immensely.

On the radio, we repeatedly heard the words "is coming, has passed, is coming, has passed", but we had no idea what that meant. Later, they played marches and read news from which we learned nothing good.

FATHER AND THE MAUSER

Father arrived later that day. I remember how he suddenly stood in front of us in knickerbockers, donning a rucksack on his back in which he only had a change of underwear, and his most personal belongings.

The most interesting item he had on him was a 10-shot Mauser pistol and extra cartridges. The 9mm Mauser was a very popular German-made gun that was also used in their army. It holds 10 bullets instead of the usual 6 or 7 in a Browning, for instance.

Seeing us stare at his pistol Father explained that he, just as all civilians, had relinquished his pistol at the outbreak of the war to arm the soldiers. But when he decided to return to Lwów, he knew that he needed a weapon to protect himself against bandits. He returned to the Warsaw police station, but there was so much chaos, he just went to the arms storage and picked the Mauser instead.

With the situation being as bad as it was, at least we were all together as a family.

Renia, age 15 (Taken in 1942)

MORE FAMILY

A few days later Mother's brother, Uncle Dziunio, his wife Jagoda and their daughter Renia arrived. They stayed in Babcia's apartment, but came upstairs for meals.

They arrived in a Fiat, but I don't remember what happened to that car. I just know they left it someplace and came back without it.

AIR RAIDS

There were several bombardments every day, but luckily none of the bombs fell in our vicinity. We spent the air raids in the basement. My parents always encouraged Wacek and me to use the hammock, but we didn't like it because it never stopped swinging. When things got really shaky, you could even fall out of it, and that happened fairly often.

Wacek despised the bombardments. During those endless hours in the basement, he tried to block the war out of his mind by studying English.

BAD NEWS

The news from the front got worse and worse. There was no indication of the desperately sought-after help from the Western allies, and even the latest gossip didn't bring any better information.

After twelve days, Lwów was surrounded by the Germans. And with that, the defense of the city began. The suburbs were under heavy artillery bombardments and their inhabitants were forced to seek refuge in the city.

BAG OF SUGAR

One of them was our friend, Professor Czekanowski. During the past few years, he had been living in the outskirts in his newly built house. The shellfire had made it dangerous to stay there, so he moved into the vacant 3-room apartment next to Babcia.

He arrived with a few things from his house and we provided him with some furniture. The most precious possession he brought with him was a 50-kilo bag of sugar.

Mother craved that bag of sugar and she never ceased to hope that she would get it as a payment for the apartment. But the bag remained in the ownership of the professor. So now, we had a non-paying, but at least quite entertaining, tenant in our house.

ATTACK ON LWÓW

The bombardments increased with each day. We spent entire days and part of the nights in the basement listening to the sound of shellfire. Luckily, the majority of the bombs fell in the direction of the citadel, which was nearby, but far enough from us.

General Sikorski and the Polish Army under his command, whom we had hoped would come and help us defend ourselves, was defeated outside the city gates of Lwów.

OFFICERS SCHOOL

The moment was approaching when Wacek was supposed to enroll in officers school. Mother did everything she could think of to dissuade him from going there. Her efforts increased dramatically when the railroad ceased to function and his only choice would have been to walk to school. In order to get there, you had to pass through Ukrainian villages. And that was extremely dangerous.

There was not a lot of love lost between the rural Ukrainians and the cosmopolitan city folk dominated by Poles and Jews. In addition, there was practically no police since the outbreak of the war. Lawlessness ruled. Chances, that peasants or robbers could mug or even murder outsiders, especially young Poles, were quite big.

Finally, Mother stopped listening to Wacek's arguments about patriotism and his national duty and flatly forbade him to go.

He was very lucky to have obeyed her, because some of his schoolmates who tried to get to the school were either killed by Ukrainians, or a few days later, caught by the Soviets who sent them to POW camps and later executed them in Katyń.

TRAGIC REACTION

On Saint Sofia Square, in a building that housed a pharmacy on the ground floor, a man jumped out the third-floor window and succumbed to his injuries.

Since all ambulances had been confiscated by the army, I don't know how they transported his body. Word had it that he was a Jew from Warsaw who couldn't accept that Lwów would be occupied by the Germans and committed suicide.

PERSONAL PERSPECTIVE

I am not recapping historical facts since they are available to anyone interested in the details. I am only limiting myself to my personal memories. Please remember that I was eleven years old at the outbreak of the war, and surely some of my recollections may be distorted.

UPPING THE ANTE

On September 17, 1939, the Soviets crossed the Polish border. It was a brutal stab in the back no one in Poland could have even dreamed of. At that time, we didn't know about the secret addition to the Soviet-German agreement. We never assumed Stalin would be willing to help Hitler with his plans.

At first, we thought the Soviets had entered Poland to help us. That was the rumor in the beginning. It didn't take long to realize that Lwów was not only left alone to defend itself against the Germans, but now also had the Soviets attacking it.

THIRD ONE OUT

The Germans and Russians began negotiations with Polish representatives. As a result, Lwów was surrendered to the Soviets on September 22. During the few hours of truce, Polish soldiers, who had already surrendered their arms, left the citadel and rushed to the city trying to hide from the Soviets by mixing with the population.

6. (1939–41)
LIVING UNDER SOVIET OCCUPATION

INVASION OF THE RED ARMY

Around three o'clock in the afternoon, we saw the first Soviet tanks rumbling down Zyblikiewicza Street, in the direction of Saint Sofia Square. We hid behind our windows and balcony doors, and cautiously watched the Soviet movements.

Red Army soldiers came down the streets pulling machine guns on wheels, while suspiciously scanning the houses as they passed by. The men were in a horrible state; unshaven, dirty, wearing filthy uniforms. It took us a moment to realize that their guns were hanging from simple twine, not leather straps like our army had.

SO-CALLED LIBERATION

It was the first sighting of our "liberators" as they liked to call themselves. With reference to this, we created the following poem:

"Liberated from the Master's chains,
From the Master's pants, from the Master's shoes
Just like the Soviet people
All we have left now is a naked ass."

FATAL MISUNDERSTANDING

On that day, next to the house of our friend, attorney Stronski, a group of people, most likely Soviet sympathizers, happily ran out into the streets when they saw the Soviet tanks approaching. They wanted to greet the Soviets and show them their appreciation.

The soldiers misunderstood their excitement and directed fire at them in response, thereby killing or wounding seven people. A big hole in the house entrance and a lot of blood on the walls remained and reminded people of what had happened.

Let's say we didn't feel sorry for them, quite the contrary. We couldn't believe that anybody could be happy over the arrival of the Soviets.

BYE, BYE SUGAR

Fearful of what the Soviets might do to his abandoned house, Professor Czekanowski gathered all his belongings, including the infamous bag of sugar, and left.

This was the end of the sugar story. For many years, we teased Mother about it.

PROLETARIAN CONDITIONS

Thus, we became part of the Red Empire. And with it came the depleted stores. Whatever had been in them before was now either sold, hidden or stolen. For those who didn't have any provisions, it was very hard to survive.

BACK TO BARTER

That's when the ancient exchange method of trading goods for food came back to life. Peasants came to town and brought us milk, cheese and sour cream just as before. Only now, they didn't take money, but wanted clothes, bed linens or other selected products instead.

Father went through our house to see what we could barter with. He had donated most of his guns to the rifle association for the defense of Lwów. But he still had a beautiful gun cover for one of his beloved guns. He traded it for some lard. The same happened to his fur hunting coat. Hania exchanged our bed sheets and pillow cases for milk, butter and sour cream.

COLOR PREFERENCE

One day the Soviets announced that the exchange rate of the Polish zloty to the Soviet ruble was set at 1:1. Now we had a new currency, but nobody wanted to take it.

Ironically, I liked the ruble bills so much for their red color, I exchanged all my savings for Russian money. But since the stores were empty and there was nothing you could buy, I just kept my cash at home.

SEVERELY ABRIDGED SHOPPING LIST

The shops were and remained literally empty – with the exception of the cheapest sort of tobacco, made from leftovers, and to go with it, you were able to buy matches and vinegar.

Bread was available from time to time, but you had to stand in long lines to "maybe" get lucky. Usually, there was only enough for the people in the very front of the line. The rest went back home empty-handed.

The search for food became the most important occupation in our lives and took up most of our time.

UNWANTED GUESTS

Since Father was unemployed, Professor Czekanowski suggested that he should contact Professor Rudolf Weigl and become his Russian interpreter. As the developer of the typhus vaccine, Weigl was a very important person for the Soviets, inasmuch as he produced what they desperately needed. Epidemics were spreading throughout the vast Soviet Union, and winter was approaching, threatening to make the desperate situation even worse.

There was a constant influx of specialists from all parts of the Soviet Empire coming to the Institute to see Weigl, but basically none of them spoke Polish. Weigl couldn't converse with his forcefully tolerated "guests" as he grew up in formerly Austrian-occupied Galicia where German was the offical language. Father on the other hand, had lived in the Russian-occupied part of Poland and was therefore forced to learn Russian

INTELLECTUAL EXCHANGE

Weigl gladly accepted Father's offer and made him his assistant. Dressed in a laboratory coat, Father was present at all meetings with Russians. I am very sorry he never wrote down his memories, because he experienced quite a lot of interesting things, including the visit of Nikita Khrushchev, who was then First Secretary of the Central Committee of the Communist Party of Ukraine, and a newly elected member of the Politburo.

Some of the visiting Soviet scientists still remembered the days when the Czar ruled Russia. Since the Russian Revolution, they had been living in intellectual isolation and were consequently very hungry to get back into contact with the world again.

LIFE UNDER STALIN

Even if these delegates were afraid of repercussions and worse, they opened up to my father; and after a few drinks, they temporarily forgot their fear and spoke very frankly about life in the Soviet Union. Father learned that things were worse there than he had ever imagined.

RULES OF SURVIVAL

Stalin had purged the Soviet army and then the Communist party apparatus by murdering everyone who was deemed not completely "loyal". It was very hard to find a safe way to survive under his regime of terror.

One of the scientists told Father in confidence that the only way you could survive life in the Soviet Union, was by not joining the Party and not stealing too much. If you joined the Party, they could kick you out. If you were kicked out, you could forget your professional career and future. If you didn't belong to the Party, there was always the hope that you would join, so you would keep your chances.

The rule about stealing was a bit different. If you stole too much, they locked you up, or killed you. If you didn't steal, you were going to die of starvation. Therefore, you had to steal, but only at a moderate rate.

I've never forgotten this advice my entire life.

IDEALISTIC VALUE

It came to Father as a great relief to be able to have work, even if the money he made in the Institute was peanuts. But we had enough money to live on as long as the zloty was valid. As a second resource, we still had plenty of goods in the house we could barter with.

PROPER BACKROUND

Wacek was already registered to study at the Technical University of Lwów. But now that the Soviets had taken control of our country, he and the other freshmen were required to pass an additional set of entry exams.

These exams were created to accept not only students with the best grades, but also those with the "right" social background. In the proletarian world of our occupiers, this meant people with a peasant and working class background.

I had to pay a different price. The Soviets required all secondary schools to employ Soviet methods of teaching.

GOOD THINKING

One day, Uncle Bogdan, who had been drafted as an officer into the Polish army, appeared at the front door. He was clad in a soldier's uniform and had broken an arm.

He had been smart to trade his officer's uniform for that of a common soldier's, otherwise he would have risked being arrested and deported by the Soviets.

BETTER IDEA

But Mother knew he wasn't safe in our home, even in those clothes. He was born in the Ukraine province, and because of his social background and being a reserve officer, he had no chance to stay.

She immediately handed him civilian clothes. After taking care of him for a few days she arranged to have him smuggled to German-occupied Warsaw where he'd have a better chance of surviving the war.

GENERAL ANDERS

In contrast to Uncle Bogdan, Uncle Żuś was a career officer. He had been wounded during the attack on Poland and was now in the hospital on Kurkowa Street. That's where many injured Polish officers were being treated, as was the later famous General Anders.

Władysław Anders had been in command of a cavalry brigade when World War II broke out. Unable to withstand the German Blitzkrieg tactics, tanks and motorized infantry, he was forced to retreat to the east. Wounded several times, Anders was taken prisoner by the Soviets and brought to Lwów. Later, he was transferred to Lubyanka prison in Moscow.

We visited Uncle Żuś in the hospital and on this occasion Father visited General Anders whom he knew from the past. General Anders was closely watched, but the lower officers like Uncle Żuś weren't.

SAVINGS LIVES

Mother insisted that Uncle Żuś get a short-term hospital leave permit to go to the city and then come to us. Żuś tried to talk her out of it, complaining how difficult it was, but Mother was very adamant. Finally, he gave in and obeyed.

He came to us a few days later. Mother immediately put him into civilian clothes, just like she did with Uncle Bogdan, sent him off after a few days to the German-occupied part of Poland, where he assumed a new name and survived the war.

Uncles Bogdan and Żuś were not the only officers who stayed at our house and whom Mother saved from the Katyń Massacre by getting them out of Soviet-occupied Poland.

EVIL EFFICIENCY

Without giving a reason, the Soviets issued an order that all officers, policemen, judges and district attorneys had to register with their local authorities.

Later, it turned out that they conveniently used this list to arrest them and their families and deport them to Kazakhstan.

WORLD UPSIDE-DOWN

Most of the people who disobeyed, unknowingly saved their own lives. Those who registered didn't stay free too long, unless they went into hiding. But that was not so easy.

There were very many spies and people who held grudges, because of "unsettled matters". It was a great time to get even with your enemy. All you had to do was to go to the Soviet authorities and denounce the person you disliked. We were not aware at that time that our janitor Janek was an informer and maybe was even collaborating with the Soviets.

SOVIET-STYLE ELECTIONS

The next chapter of our Soviet occupation began with the so-called "elections". The issue at stake was whether a pretext could be manufactured that we wanted to become part of the Soviet Union. It was a joke, just as all Soviet elections were.

WAVING THE CARROT

As this election was arranged for quickly, the Soviets weren't well prepared. In the elections that followed they always stocked the ballot locations with goods that previously hadn't been available, to better "motivate" people to cast their ballot. But at our first Soviet-style election, they didn't even have the famous election kiełbasa (Polish sausage) to spark our enthusiasm.

We had the "choice" to elect one – and only one candidate who later voted "in our name" that we wanted to become citizens of the Soviet Union. There were some official manifestations to underline the popularity of his goal. With no seeming opposition, we consequently became Soviet citizens.

CLOSE ESCAPE

In late Fall, Uncle Dziunio, Mother's brother, decided he wanted to fight our enemies from the outside, and join the Polish Army in exile in France.

In order to get there, he had to illegally leave Poland via Hungary. Mother gave him money and a change of clothes. He received our blessings and set off with a group of similarly-minded people.

LAST POINT OF RETURN

To our surprise, he knocked on our door a few days later. His group hadn't noticed that they were being watched by the NKVD. During their train ride to the Hungarian border, Uncle got suspicious and claimed he needed to go to the toilet. But instead of going into the restroom, he opened the exit door and jumped out of the moving train, just before they arrived at the station where the entire group was arrested.

A few days later, he took his wife and daughter and illegally left the Soviet-occupied zone to seek refuge in the German-occupied zone.

DAVID AND GOLIATH

In November 1939, the Soviets attacked Finland. This act made Stalin the laughing stock of the entire world. Just as when Goliath attacked little David, this small country refused to give in, but continued to fight as long as they could.

Finland's small army of 200,000 men exposed the state of the Soviet Union's poorly trained and miserably equipped Red Army. It wasn't until March 1940 that the Finnish government had to sign a peace treaty, and by that surrendered 16,000 square miles of territory to the Soviet Union.

Of course, the Soviet propaganda lied as usual. They never admitted their failure.

SCREWED-UP SYSTEM

The Soviets came to our country with the intention to force a six-day week on us. It didn't take long until they realized that it didn't work and returned to the normal seven-day week calendar.

BEING CRAFTY

The imposition of a six-day week and its subsequent revocation affected our school system and caused problems, like with the newly introduced "dziennik" or grade book.

The dziennik was a Soviet scholastic control instrument that we always had to have with us and take home to get it signed by our parents once a week. With this grade book, our parents were always on the ball about how we were progressing in our studies.

The return to the seven-day week made the Soviet, six-day-based dziennik unusable. As a consequence, we had to make a new grade book by hand.

COMPLEX ISSUES

Another change that was far more drastic was the removal of our curriculum, Polish school and exercise books, without providing us with an alternative. The new method was to take notes of each lesson and study from them. This brought about a shortage of notebooks. But before we could get a new one, we had to hand in the old one. This was quite absurd, because we needed the old ones to keep up with our studies.

To make matters worse, the only writing utensils available were violet ink and the dreaded chemical pencils, which made writing a messy endeavor.

IN THE SAME BOAT

Our teachers were no better off than we. They had no knowledge of the Soviet teaching system and had to work their way through this chaotic situation as well.

To top things off, the school didn't get any coal to heat the class rooms, so we went to lessons dressed in winter coats, hats and gloves.

SURPRISE!

A day before Christmas Eve, our currency, the Polish zloty, was suddenly no longer valid. It was only accepted in the German-occupied zone. But that was of no help to us.

SMART MOVE

Hardly anybody had Russian money beyond some small change – except for me, for the simple reason that I found the ruble bills so red and pretty. And thanks to this move, I became rich!

The abolition of our national currency started my "career" as the banker of the house. I gave out loans to the family. In this way, I ensured that we had quite a nice Christmas and could feed our many guests.

SOVIET JUSTICE

The day after Christmas, a Ukrainian and a Jewish representative of the Soviet authorities knocked on our door and told Mother that they had come "to turn her into a beggar".

Under Soviet rule, our houses were to be nationalized, our silver and jewelry and all other valuables "given back to the people" since we had defrauded the poor to get them in the first place.

WRONG PERSON TO PICK ON

Father was not at home, but Mother was not a person who was easily intimidated. She immediately started an argument.

Before she let them in, she demanded they identify themselves with proper official documentation. There was only a small problem. She couldn't read or understand Russian or Ukrainian, so the argument went on for quite some time.

THE UNDER-THE-SKIRT TRICK

In the meanwhile, Hania quickly collected our most valuable items, hid them in her skirt and snuck them out of the apartment unnoticed.

By the time the confiscators were finally let in, Mother could prove that she didn't own anything of value, and what she had, she had to sell to buy food to feed the family. During their argument, Father came home. As he spoke Russian, he gave them a speech which they didn't understand. The duped men had no other choice than to leave empty handed.

JUST CAUSE

Four days later, on New Year's Eve, Mother joyously threw a big "Saint Sylvester" party with plenty of food and drink she had bought earlier when these goods were still available.

This is how the New Year of 1940 began.

FROSTBITE

It was an extremely cold winter. In order to buy food, you had to stand in line for hours and even days. To brave the sub-zero temperatures, I wore Father's hunting boots. They were the best I had, but even they didn't help avoid getting my feet frostbitten. Because frostbite couldn't be treated immediately and properly, the damage became permanent. Even today, I can still feel the effects of it.

CHANGES, CHANGES

The first news upon my return from winter break was that our classroom was moved to the high school Wacek previously attended. The bad news was that 6th grade was degraded to 5th grade in Soviet school terms, because their system only consisted of ten years instead of our twelve years in Poland. The first year of Gymnasium, that is 7th grade, was also "demoted" to 5th grade. 8th grade was morphed into 6th grade, and so on. It felt very strange, as if we had failed class and had to repeat the year, or even two.

MAKING THE BEST OF THINGS

The temperature was often so low that we didn't have classes in our unheated school. On those days, we went skiing instead.

CLUTCHING AT ANY STRAW

Father was very interested in politics and was hungry for every bit of information.

Unfortunately, there wasn't any good news about our future. In order to survive the war psychologically, we had to find reasons to cheer us up. People began speculating about the value of the "Wernyhora Prophecy" and other similar stories that helped us keep our spirits at a better level.

WERNYHORA

Wernyhora was a legendary poet and prophet from the Ukrainian region of 18th-century Poland who predicted that Poland would be resurrected as a nation.

The rebirth was associated with the Old Polish-Lithuanian Commonwealth which included the Ukraine and represented a very romantic idea of Poland, as held by many Poles.

DREAM ON, DAD

Father kept his faith focused on the day the British would land in Baku on the Caspian Sea and cut off the Soviet's access to oil, which as a result would then force them to surrender.

I don't know why or where he got these ideas, but they were very often debated.

EVENING OF THE THREE KINGS

I remember the day our school went to see Shakespeare's Evening of the Three Kings. The play was staged in the small and cozy, formerly Jewish, now Polish theater on Jagiellońska Street.

THE REAL WORLD

On our way to the theatre, we passed a group of prisoners guarded by the NKVD. It was very depressing and instead of watching the performance, my mind was with those men. I worried about what was going to happen to them and feared the worst.

This was my first encounter with a reality I had so far only heard about. Every day, somebody was arrested, but I personally had never seen how people were torn away from their lives simply because they were considered unwelcome or dangerous elements in the world of our occupiers.

FIRST WAVE OF MASS DEPORTATIONS

At the end of January or the beginning of February 1940, when the temperatures were extremely low, the Soviets began mass deportations to Siberia.

The majority of the victims were farmers, formerly Polish soldiers who had been settled in eastern Poland to live in the predominantly Ukrainian villages in order to keep them under control. They were very patriotic people and therefore dangerous elements in Soviet terms.

We heard about this wave of deportations, but we never saw it happen.

NOW LWÓW

In the beginning of April, organized deportations began in Lwów. Late at night small trucks – built in a factory established by the Ford Motor Company – rumbled through the streets, each loaded with a few soldiers and a commander.

MERCILESS JOURNEY

These groups entered the homes of selected people and gave them only a short time to gather their personal belongings. The soldiers were often brutal and forced the victims at gunpoint into the truck.

The deportees were brought to the freight railroad station and loaded into old, unheated cattle cars. The journey to one of the many villages in Kazakhstan. Without food, water or sanitary facilities, it swas so brutal that many people died along the way.

TICKING TIME BOMB

Since many of my schoolmates and friends were deported during this wave, we were terrified that we would be next.

My parents prepared suitcases filled with our most necessary belongings, so in case the NKVD stood in front of our door one night, we would just have to grab them and not waste valuable time.

BRIEF RESPITE

In order to better cope with this permanent fear, people passed by the NKVD office at a certain time of the day to see whether a line of those dreaded small trucks were standing ready for a new round-up and whether soldiers exited the building in groups.

If all was calm, they returned home with the good news that this night they could most likely rest peacefully.

We were gratefully spared from deportation.

SOVIET CITIZENSHIP

The next stage of the occupation was the introduction of so-called "Soviet passports", which were actually just identification papers. The moment you picked them up from the authorities, you automatically became a citizen of the Soviet Union.

I was the only one in the family who didn't have to pick up such a document, because I wasn't 16 years old yet, which was the minimum age for those papers.

BLAST FROM THE PAST

Mother was in a foul mood when she was called to get her passport. Her anger quickly turned into fear when she realized that the militiaman, who handed out her passport was no other than our former house painter, Gołębiowski

He recognized her, too. When he greeted her with the ominous words: "So here we meet again, Comrade Szybalska" and gave her the passport with a smirk. Her heart dropped.

By the time Mother had returned home, she was distraught. She was afraid her day of reckoning had come.

PARAGRAPH ELEVEN

And it did. Shortly after, my family got an order to return to the passport office to get the "paragraph 11" annotation stamped into their new passports. Paragraph 11, or the so-called "wolves ticket", prohibited you from living in a border area or any bigger city. And that included Lwów.

Just the thought of having to leave the apartment and Lwów and move to some small village where there was no place to live and no place for Father to work caused us great worry. It would be terrible.

WITH THE HELP OF A FRIEND

Father took advantage of his connections to Professor Weigl. Together, they went to the regional party committee and after a very long and tedious discussion, the authorities finally withdrew the dreaded paragraph 11, thereby sparing us from having to leave our home.

SAD SMOCZEK

After the family of one of Leszek's friend's was deported to Kazakhstan, my cousin got an orphaned Dachshund named Smoczek.

Leszek took good care of him. Smoczek was a sweet, but very sad dog, because he missed his owners. We did our best to cheer him up by taking him for long walks, running and playing with him and spoiling him with all sorts of snacks.

His legs were very short and his belly hung so low, it touched the pavement. When it rained, his belly got so dirty we had to give him a bath.

Leszek didn't like the janitor of his building. Every time Smoczek lifted his leg to pee when he left the house, Leszek tore on the leash dragging the poor dog away as quickly as he could. As a result Smoczek sprayed urine all along the sidewalk.

I don't know whether this upset the janitor or not. We never found out.

Leszek and his mother

RUSSIAN NEIGHBORS

In the meantime, the Soviets confiscated a room in Babcia's two-room apartment. She had already been sharing her place with Kasia, a friend of Uncle Dziunio. Kasia was a big land owner from the Poznań region and the wife of Dziunio's army colleague.

The room was given to a very polite Russian – a Jewish commander called Zołotów. At first, everything seemed fine, but then his wife followed shortly after and the commander then felt that living in one small walk-through room was not enough anymore.

He "suggested" that Grandmother and Kasia move into the small room and he would take the bigger room with his wife. Babcia really didn't have a choice.

EVERYTHING IS RELATIVE

The fact that Babcia's apartment didn't have a kitchen, but just a burner in the bathroom didn't bother the Zołotów back home they were used to much worse conditions.

Babcia was fluent in Russian and she learned a lot of about life in the Soviet Union from them. In return, the couple was eager to find out how life had been in Poland before the outbreak of the war. They talked a lot, especially after a few drinks. And the Zołotóws could get very drunk.

FAMILY AFFAIR

The Soviet authorities returned to our house with the intention of boarding a second officer, this time in our apartment. In the end, Father made a deal that we would move Babcia and Kasia into my parent's bedroom and vacate the room downstairs. This way, we were able to avoid having a total stranger put in our midst.

Mother and I moved into the living room and Father put up an iron bed in the dining room. In those days, married people of our class often did not share a bedroom; everybody had their own bedroom. Wacek stayed in his room, which was a walk-through to Babcia's new bedroom. This is how we lived until the time we left Lwów.

GERMAN SHOPPING SPREE

In the spring of 1940, a German commission to repatriate Germans from the Soviet occupation came to Lwów. I remember how the German members of the commission loved to go to the delicatessen. They bought up everything they could get and which was too expensive for us, like smoked fish, caviar, champagne and other spirits.

WISHFUL THINKING

In addition to Germans seeking repatriation, they also registered people from western Poland who wanted to return to their homes.

Although the Germans nicely registered these people, hardly anyone received permission to return.

Another group of people eager to get registered were Jews who had enough of the Soviets and wanted to return to their pre-war apartments and houses. They didn't believe the Germans would murder them. This was before the first Jewish Ghettoes were created.

CRUEL TRICK

Those who registered with the Germans indirectly admitted that they didn't support the Soviet system. According to our Soviet occupiers, these people were proven "unreliable".

A year later, Soviet authorities used this registration list to deport all of them to Kazakhstan.

TWIST OF FATE

As strange as it may have seemed then, the deportation turned out to be the lesser of two evils for many of the Jews. They were not sent to German concentration camps, but returned to Poland after the war. Some even made a career taking high positions under Poland's Communist regime, especially in key positions of the security forces and the army.

POLITICAL CATASTROPHY

All local events were completely moved to the back burner of public interest the moment Norway and then France capitulated.

Many Poles were fighting in France in the hope of defeating Hitler from there. Polish troops also landed in Narvik, Norway as part of an expeditionary force in an effort to save Norway, but they failed. Many Poles were killed in the battle and buried in what then became a Polish cemetery there.

We had reached the end of all our hope. There was nothing good to expect after that.

ANTOHER BLOW

The Soviets installed a Russian as the new director of the Typhus Institute. With a Russian as his superior, Professor Weigl no longer needed Father as his translator.

As if things weren't bad enough, the new director moved into an apartment in our house, so he could keep an even closer eye on us.

Without missing an opportunity to help his friend, Weigl created a job just for Father. He was "promoted" and made transport manager of the Institute's carport. The war bonded the two men even closer. Their friendship remained till the end of their lives.

NEWS FROM THE FREE WORLD

Father often spent evenings with the professor discussing politics. They listened to the news from London every day, and Father used it as the basis of his political analysis.

We often laughed and joked that Father was becoming what one would call today "a homemade political analyst".

His forte was his adamant determination to hold on to his wishful thoughts, when actually there was no hope left.

FLEXIBILITY REQUIRED

There were a lot of changes in my school. Wacek's former arts and crafts teacher was now teaching me algebra. And our neighbor from St. Marek Street, who gave my brother singing lessons and was a pharmacist by profession, was now teaching us Russian.

LEARNING RUSSIAN

I was lucky that Father, who was fluent in Russian, could help me. Otherwise, I would never have been able to learn the language. It was also fortunate that my Russian school teacher was very understanding and good-hearted, so I managed to get by.

ANCIENT HISTORY

I was less fortunate in my ancient history class. Our teacher was a Ukrainian who was bald and had a very small head. We gave him the moniker, "Skull", referring to the emblem the SS wore on their hats.

Skull forced us to work with school books written in Ukrainian which I didn't understand. He constantly made us write exams and gave out bad grades, and if someone didn't understand him, all hell broke loose. From that time on, I hated ancient history.

In the end, I finished fifth grade for the second time, that is, the Soviet 5th grade, with acceptable grades.

KRAKIDAŁY

Since the money Father was making was not enough to support the family, we had to sell whatever we had at the flea market. The good thing was that we still had many possessions that were very marketable.

To get to the flea market, we took the street car to the Grand Theater. Behind it was a large space we called "Krakidały" or "On Paris".

We sold our goods on the sidewalk. Quite often, you had to fight for each meter as there were too many vendors and not enough space.

FUNNY SIDE OF THINGS

Selling goods there was an unforgettable experience; some incidents were quite funny and should be made into a film or at least be compiled in a book.

Most of the people inspecting goods were Soviets. They bought all sorts of things, some of them for unusual and even absurd reasons.

RUSSIAN-STYLE OUTING

One item I recall was Polish ladies' nightgowns. Soviets loved to buy them for their women who wore them as evening gowns when going to the opera or theater.

Many years later, when I was doing business in Moscow, I had a female translator – whom I suspected was a KGB informant – and whose other duty was to keep an eye on me.

In a rare moment of truth, she told me how her mother, who, as she defined, was "of better standing", laughed at this so-called elegance, because "of course" she knew that these dresses were actually nightgowns and not evening attire.

CUSTOMER IS THE BOSS

Very popular among the Soviets were also old postcards which they misinterpreted as art and hung on the wall to embellish their homes.

Old toys, especially mechanical ones, bedding and many other small things also sold quickly and got a good price. We spent many evenings at the flea market in the summer helping to increase our household money.

ACCEPTING ONE'S FATE

In the fall of 1940, you could say that our little world had leveled out into a state of calm. We slowly started to accept our plight of having to live under foreign occupation and didn't expect any changes soon.

My father continued to predict that the Soviet alliance with the Germans would change, but at that time, friendship and love between Stalin and Hitler were still blooming. The Soviets continued to supply Germany with war-time raw materials without interruption.

EASY WINTER

Schools were still unheated, but that winter it wasn't as cold, so it wasn't as bad as the winter of 1939/40.

MINOR RESTRICTIONS

I went swimming in an indoor pool and sometimes skiing in our park or ice-skating on the ice rink.

Unfortunately, our usual ice-skating rink wasn't accessible. It was too close to the NKVD building and also closed, so we had to go to a rink that was much further away.

RECYCLED PANTS

I was proud of my new pair of ski pants. They were made from the army pants Uncle Bogdan had left behind when he changed into civilian clothes.

As these were not a pair of officer uniform pants, but of a regular soldier, the material was hard and tough like leather. They were perfect as ski pants, and I wore them for many, many years.

7. (1941)
CHANGE OF THE GUARDS

CHECK POINT

During summer break, Leszek and I often went on bicycle excursions to the outskirts of Lwów. We wanted to learn more about the countryside which was completely unknown to us.

On June 21st, 1941, on our way back home from Skniłów, not far from the airport, we were startled to see a Soviet army check-point set up in front of us.

Soldiers checked all cars and horse-driven carts, but did not ask us for papers. It was rather surprising to us, since this roadblock hadn't been here a couple of hours earlier when we passed by.

BAD SIGN?

As soon as I returned home, I told the family about it. Father started to deliberate about the reason for this. Was it because they were preparing a new deportation wave to Kazakhstan as the pessimists were constantly predicting?

EARLY MORNING SURPRISE

The following day was Sunday. It was the only day we could sleep as long as we wanted. But this morning Wacek tore us out of our sleep before 5 a.m. to tell us that he heard German airplanes in the air.

At first we tried to ignore him, but then Father turned on the radio and found a German station that broadcast a live speech by Joseph Goebbels. He had a recognizable voice that drove chills down your spine. Hitler's propaganda minister informed the world that Germany had declared war on the Soviet Union.

In the meanwhile, Soviet civilians had already armed themselves and begun evacuating.

SURVIVAL OF THE FITTEST

Even though my life's experience was rather slim, I immediately sensed that another perfect moment for great business deals had just arisen – if I acted quickly.

After having seen that any kind of savings bank was a very unwise place to keep money, I had withdrawn all of mine and stored it in my room.

In addition to my cash, I borrowed all of my brother's savings under the condition that I would return his money in the ratio 1:1 of the currency that would be introduced after the Germans took over.

PRAISE 24/7!

It was Sunday, very early in the morning and all the stores were closed – with the exception of the big "Gastronom" delicatessen which was open 24 hours a day. The delicatessen was located in the former Zalewski Chocolate Store. The original owner Mr. Zalewski had been arrested by the Soviets and – so I heard – killed in one of the Soviet detention centers.

RIGHT PLACE AT THE RIGHT TIME

I took Father's backpack and hurried to the delicatessen. I don't believe that anybody shopping or working in the store had any idea that the German attack on the Soviet Union had begun.

I acted as inconspicuously as I could, but I really didn't have to worry. They just saw in me a 13-year-old boy with a backpack. Most likely, they thought I was the son of a farmer making some early morning purchases. I quickly gathered everything that had a good market value: cigarettes, cans, chocolates and candy.

I spent all my money.

POKER FACE WINS

I played my cards well. sLater, I found out that on cigarettes alone I earned enough money to pay back my debts, purchase some good-quality material and pay the tailor for my very own first bespoken suit!

I gave Mother a lot of cans to contribute to the family household. Then, I set up my own "store" on a shelf in the salon, which was now my room, and sold my goods to people who came by. The proceeds from this I kept as pocket money.

·

REASON TO REJOICE

After returning home, I found my family gleefully standing on the balcony. They were watching the Soviets, panic written on their faces, rushing to leave town before the Germans reached Lwów.

During the day, more and more friends dropped in to celebrate the departure of our enemies. We stood on the balcony bidding the despised Soviets farewell and toasting that our houses would be returned to us soon, as the Germans arrived which we estimated was going to be in a few hours.

LAUGHING AT THE LOSERS

The Soviets had hardly left, when jokes mocking their desolate world started popping up everywhere, such as this one:

*"How many people do you need
to man a Soviet tank?"*

*"You need 103 people –
3 people sitting inside
and 100 to move the damn thing."*

While we were making fun of the Soviets fleeing in panic, two years of everyday terror was forgotten momentarily. We forgot that the Germans were also enemies, and could be even worse than the Soviets, but in that moment it wasn't important. We were so happy to see our occupiers go.

Little did we know that Soviet brutality was going to return for a brief time – and with a vengeance.

THE NICE NKVD CHAUFFEUR

Commander Zołotów and his wife had departed before we knew it, as did the NKVD chauffeur who lived in Count Łozinski's apartment one floor above us.

After the Soviets occupied Finland in 1940, the NKVD came to arrest the Count as he was an honorary consul to Finland and consequently became an enemy of the Soviets. But when they saw how old and sick the Count was, they changed their approach and moved their driver into his apartment to watch over him instead. The chauffeur was very polite to us and always had a smile on his face.

BACK TO THE BASEMENT

If I remember correctly, we experienced one or two bombardments. They both fell on the citadel. During the night, we had another bombardment, and spent the rest of the night in the basement.

APPEARANCES CAN BE DECEITFUL

The following days were very similar. On Thursday, it looked like the Germans were just about to enter the city. Suddenly, we saw our so-called friendly NKVD chauffeur return. He was wearing his work suit. At first, we couldn't figure out what was different, but we realized that it was drenched with blood. He wordlessly returned to his apartment, washed, changed and left for the last time.

Later, we learned that most of the Soviets had left the city, but since the Germans hadn't yet entered, they returned to "clean up" and literally massacred thousands of Polish and Ukrainian inmates in the overfilled prisons.

Only then did we understand that the red stains on the seemingly friendly driver's clothes were human blood and he had been one of those brutal slaughterers.

NEW HELPERS

On Friday, Ukrainian sharpshooters entered the city. They forced their way into the top-floor homes to take up positions and shoot at Soviet soldiers in the streets.

An armored car with loudspeakers mounted on its roof drove through the streets and ordered us to shut our windows and doors, and threatened that if there was any movement they would shoot without any warning or explanation.

It was very hot that day, but we had no choice but to comply with those orders.

WAR ZONE

Shortly after, Soviet soldiers who had remained in the city and had been monitoring the streets entered the houses to kill the Ukrainian sharpshooters.

The situation was chaotic, and often they shot innocent people, too.

The situation was similar on Saturday and Sunday. Bombardments continued sporadically. We had to spend part of the day and the entire night in the basement.

On Monday morning, things started to become very quiet. Very brave people went out on the street to see what was happening.

8. (1941–43)
NOW, THE GERMAN
VERSION

FIRST IMPRESSION

The first German detachments that entered Lwów were mountain troops with "Edelweiss" flowers emblems on their hats. Most of them were actually Austrians who behaved very friendly to the population.

People cheered the troops in the streets. They were treated as liberators and greeted with flowers. Most of these enthusiasts were Ukrainians who believed that the Germans would allow them to build a free and independent Ukrainian State.

SHOWING THEIR TRUE FACE

On Thursday, the Einsatzgruppe SS, i.e. a special detachment of the SS, came to Lwów. They were accompanied by Ukrainians from the Nachtigall [Nightingale (sic!)] Battalion and were armed with lists that they used to immediately arrest Polish professors from Lwów University, the Technical University, the Veterinary Academy and the Academy of Foreign Trade.

We later learned that 40 professors and their families, with the exception of Professor Groer, our pediatrician, were murdered that night.

So the so-called liberators didn't waste any time introducing themselves as they really were.

TO KEEP, OR NOT KEEP

As I mentioned before, the apartment across from us had been occupied by the Soviet director of the Typhus Institute. For the sake of peace and to get on his good side, we loaned him a lot of household goods. It wasn't a big issue, we had enough, anyway.

Now that he had escaped, we wanted to retrieve our things. We carefully climbed over our joint kitchen balcony into his apartment. We had to admit that the apartment was in a very orderly state because, as we had learned previously, they didn't own too many things to begin with.

We saw that the Russian had taken all of his personal belongings, and most of the objects we loaned them. Hania was very upset. As compensation, he left us a lot of books, mostly Soviet propaganda, as well as writings by Lenin and Stalin printed on onion skin.

For the next few years, we used these books as our toilet paper and sometimes as toilet literature.

SMOKING CIGARETTES

In the summer of 1941, Operation Barbarossa was well underway. The situation at the front required a lot of changes. There were a lot of German soldiers swarming around everywhere.

Leszek and I went to a wild, uninhabited area to watch the troops moving. I had brought a pack of cigarettes with me. If I remember correctly, they were called Aftomachina which is "car" in Russian. They were very popular cigarettes, thick as a finger and the favorite brand among truck drivers. We lit up our cigarettes and smoked.

BAD, EITHER WAY

Even though I didn't inhale, it was all over after a few drags. I felt nauseous and got a terrible headache. All I wanted to do was go home and lie down.

Nothing happened to Leszek – that was the beginning of a serious habit that he couldn't kick, even on his death bed half a century later.

The moment Hania saw my green face she immediately put me to bed and brought me warm tea. I really had a terrible time, but eventually I fell asleep. This was the end of my second, very short experiment with smoking.

BELLA ITALIA

A few days later, Italians marched into Lwów. Germany's allies made our city their headquarters, and set up their own hospital here.

The apartment across from ours was now occupied by two Italian officers. I remember them so well. Aldo Catriani was a physician and Luigi Niti, a carabinieri captain.

Several soldiers moved in shortly after, followed by quite a few pretty young Jewish girls who they hid in their apartment.

We had a good relationship with our charming neighbors. We communicated with them thanks to my brother who spoke Italian and functioned as our translator. I remember they gave us coal and Mother baked them a big cake.

This idyllic relationship lasted until July 1943, when our friendly occupiers were called back to Italy. We were very sad to see them go. We had tears in our eyes when they departed.
As did their ladies.

I don't know what happened to them. After the war, when I was in Italy, I tried to locate them with the help of my Italian friends, but unfortunately I was unsuccessful.

ANOTHER SLAUGHTERING

Not long after they left, Italy surrendered.

In Lwów, the Germans took revenge on their former allies who surrendered to the Allies. For this act of treason it was said that they murdered 15.000 Italian officers. The executions took place on the "Sands", the same grounds on which they murdered Jews.

BACK TO BASICS AGAIN

After the shop owners had sold all their food supplies, the shelves remained empty as new deliveries never arrived.

Money had become worthless, so we had to resort to barter, again. Peasants came to town to trade their produce for household and industrial goods. We luckily still had goods and didn't have problems procuring food.

The biggest difficulty was to buy bread and sugar. It required standing in long lines for hours, which wasn't as bad as previously under Soviet occupation, since it was summer and during the long waits we would meet new acquaintances and make new friends.

We helped each other in keeping our place in the queue, and learned to make the best of the situation.

RARE EXCEPTION

There was one store which had a lot of goods, but no customers; it was the school physics instrumentation supply store on Akademicka Street.

This shop became Wacek's favorite hangout. The prices were rock bottom to attract at least a few customers. In addition, it was summer break, so there was literally zero demand for school supplies.

In order to sell any merchandise at all, the store manager lowered the prices even more. This was the moment Wacek moved in. He bought, among other things, a car battery, an electric charger, a big transformer, lamps with nickel-cadmium batteries and many other useful objects.

Thanks to his ingenuity, we were later able to overcome many problems when life became a notch more difficult.

OFF LIMITS

Żelazna Woda, our local swimming place, was now "off limits" to us and only open to the Germans. The only pool we were allowed to swim in was quite far away.

The better alternative was a clay pit filled with rain water nearby. Since the water was stagnant, it was surely loaded with bacteria, but at that time we didn't care too much about that. We were more concerned about not getting caught by the Germans.

If they found us, they would arrest us and then send us to a German labor camp.

ÜBERMENSCH IDEOLOGY

According to Hitler's Germanic expansion ideology, Poles were to be kept "stupid". A dumb society is much easier to rule.

As a consequence of this belief, the German occupiers closed all schools except for grammar and vocational schools, and tried to entice young Poles to go to Germany to work.

AT THE TYPHUS INSTITUTE

Professor Weigl's Institute was put under the Chief Command of the German Army. His vaccine against typhus was also highly sought after by the new occupying force. They desperately needed the vaccine for their soldiers on the front where the hygienic situation was deplorable and the increase in typhus cases was already creating strategic problems.

As the Institute's cars had been taken by the departing Soviets, Father's position as car park manager had become obsolete. With little other choice, he became one of the many hundreds, and by the end of the war, thousands, of so-called human lice feeders a job which he later paid for with tuberculosis and an early death.

The job as a lice feeder[1] was to provide his or her legs to which 7 - 11 lice-filled cages were placed. The lice would then stick their heads through the cage's screen bottom, pierce the feeder's skin and suck his or her blood for about 45 minutes. The lice were cultivated to produce typhus fever vaccine.

1: Find out more about the lice feeder at http://if-show.de/Lice-Feeder

LICE CAN SAVE LIVES

Wacek began to work as a lice feeder manager and Father became one of his feeders.

The Institute offered the best documents available for the population. They were given out by the chief Commander of the German Army. These papers protected Weigl's employees from arrest by the local police, deportation to Germany and even death.

In the beginning, these papers also made available better food rations, similar to those they gave out to the German soldiers. Thanks to them, we had more food available.

ANY SCHOOL IS BETTER THAN NO SCHOOL

Since my school no longer existed, I was registered for a two-year program at a commercial school for small business people. The school was located in a run-down building in the old city. Nuns ran a soup kitchen for the poor on the ground floor.

I was one of the youngest students. The others were much older and more experienced in the business field. Most of them were already selling and buying in various markets. The only reason they were here was to have the obligatory papers that would exempt them from being sent to forced labor in Germany.

STORES ONLY FOR GERMANS

One of my fellow students was a boy who was training in one of the Meinl stores. Meinl was an elegant grocery-coffee chain from Austria that already existed in Lwów before the war.

NEW RULES

Mother never shopped there. And now, if she wanted to, she couldn't.

Meinl was now exclusively open to Germans. It was illegal to shop there for a non-German and if you were caught there, you were severely punished.

Some of my classmates adapted to the new rules and dealt in German food stamps that were given out to "German nationals only". They stood in front of these stores and bought the stamps from the Germans, with which they then bought food for resale. It was illegal and a risky business, but it was tolerated to a certain point.

PERSONAL VENDETTA

After the war, when I traveled to Austria and Germany, I often passed by Meinl stores. But I never entered one again. I decided that since they didn't let us buy their products during the war, I was never going to set foot into one of their stores now. I am aware that this wasn't even a drop in the bucket, but at least I could exercise my own private boycott and express my feelings.

Later, I learned that Julius Meinl III, who was married to a Jew, fled to Britain when the Nazis annexed Austria in 1938. The trademark "Meinl" was misappropriated during Nazi rule until Julius returned after the war to rebuild his family's retail empire. Meinl lost its shine when his grandson not only drove the coffee-roasting chain into the ground, but finally sullied the family name when he was arrested in Vienna on suspicion of defrauding investors through secretive share buybacks.

Ironically, the last, a few traditional Meinl stores can be found – of all places – in Poland!

THE ONION SKIN METHOD

My studies weren't very interesting. The curriculum was geared for people who wanted to become sales clerks and lacked other ambitions. Moreover, many of the subjects were old-fashioned and sometimes even funny.

For instance, they didn't teach us how to type, because they didn't have any typewriters. Instead, they taught us how to write letters with a chemical pencil and then copy them into a book made of onion skin pages.

In order to make a copy, you had to moisten the onion skin so that the ink could make an imprint on it. This was a slightly outdated method, but since they didn't have typewriters or carbon paper, this was the only alternative for making copies.

GOING TO THE MOVIES

After having endured two years of Soviet propaganda and very poor quality films, the Germans curiously allowed the screening of pre-war Polish movies.

We immediately ran to the cinema. It was a big attraction. The movie theatres also showed German propaganda, anti-Polish and anti-Semitic movies, but we didn't watch any of those.

SNEAKY PLAN UNCOVERED

Our brief moment of joy ended abruptly when we found out that the profits from our movie tickets were being used to help finance the German war machine.

The saying "Only pigs go to the movies" spread like wildfire. It goes without saying that we stopped going to the cinema.

FAVORITE SUBJECTS

Among all the boring subjects they taught in business school, I found business algebra interesting, as well as shorthand, although I didn't stick to it until the end.

The things I learned in business algebra, I still know and use today. Our teacher, Mr. Rawicz, whom we suspected was Jewish, taught us how to simplify accounting in such a way that you could calculate everything in your head without using pen and paper. His method was very simple, but extremely useful.

I also liked chemistry where I learned a lot about product materials and their chemical contents.

CALCULATING YOUR CHANGES

I was only one of a few students who attended all lectures. The other students were there as little as possible since they were all working the markets and had no time to attend school. They had to figure out how many hours they had to be present in order not to get expelled, because in that case the school would have to notify the employment office. Once your name was listed there, you would most likely be sent to Germany to work in the German industries which were constantly getting bombed by the western allies.

BORDERS WITHIN POLAND

Lwów became the capital of the "Galizien" district and by this, also part of the so-called Général Gouvernement. This meant that we were not annexed by the Germans, but managed under German administration with Polish help.

This distinction brought about several differences: while the Général Gouvernement used the so-called Polish navy-blue police, the Galician district employed Ukrainian police, who were very unpleasant, especially to the non-Ukrainian population. For some time, the border between the old German demarcation line remained, and we needed a special permit to cross this border.

As I recently learned from an American documentary, in 1939–40, before Hitler's attack on the Soviet Union and the establishment of the "Galizien", Germans considered the Général Gouvernement a dumping ground for Poles from territories which became part of Germany, but who couldn't be "Germanized".

BLACK MARKET HUB

There was a very poor supply of necessities in Lwów, so the most important products had to be smuggled from the rest of Poland. This was done by either Germans or German businessmen who collaborated with Poles to make money.

TEMPTATION OF COLOR

During the Soviet occupation, things had been very grey. Everything was grey. The stores have been very simple and completely lacked any kind of decoration.

When the Germans took over, they opened stores that were elegantly and tastefully furnished just as it was before the war.

I remember an office supply store that opened on the corner of Jagiellońska and May 3rd Street. It displayed beautiful stationeries, and even fountain pens and pencils in the window. They had everything you could dream of.

DREAM BUBBLE BURSTS

I came by a few days later with all my savings and a long list of the wonderful things I wanted to buy. Just as I was about to enter the store, I found a sign on the door indicating that the store was now off-limits to non-Germans. This brought my shopping spree to a brutal halt.

GERMANS FIRST

The same thing happened to other stores the Germans opened – they too were restricted only to German customers. As for us, all we got were what the Soviets left behind – empty shelves and the black market.

TIT FOR TAT

But the black market often offered better quality merchandise and food than the Germans got with their food ration cards. So we probably ate much better than they did. Of course, the situation was entirely different for poor people. They didn't have the means to buy things on the black market. They had no possibility to compensate for this discrimination.

VOLKSDEUTSCHE

We began to notice a new group of people appearing in our midst, the so-called Volksdeutsche. They were people who had some German blood in their line of heritage, but didn't have German citizenship. The neighbor whom you knew as a Pole yesterday could suddenly present himself as a Volksdeutsch the next day. We used to say they were selling their souls for white bread. An old poem was modified to describe our attitude towards these people:

"Who are you, you little Volksdeutsch?
What is your motto?
White bread.
Who made you?
The situation of the war.
What is your death?
A dry tree branch.
What is your grave?
Just bare soil.
What is your monument?
A pile of shit. "

VISIT TO THE GHETTO

In the fall of 1941, Professor Weigl sent Father to Warsaw. The German authorities granted Father official approval to travel there. Little did they know that the reason for his journey was to smuggle vaccine – which had been siphoned off in the Institute under the eyes of the Germans – and bring it to the Warsaw Ghetto where an outbreak of a typhus epidemic was imminent.

LITTLE ROOSTERS

Father successfully fulfilled his mission and returned from this trip with a lot of different goods that weren't available in Lwów. Among other things, he brought razor blades and headache medicine which was very popular in Poland before the war; it was called "Little Roosters", because that was the company's trademark.

My school buddies and I worked very hard to sell these items at a good price, so Father could recoup the money he invested for the purchases and make a little profit.

SIDE JOBS

To be frank, I don't know how he was able to support us. His income as a lice feeder was so meager we never could have survived on it. He began to trade diamonds, oriental carpets, antique watches – whatever he could get his hands on.

From time to time, Mother would sell a few of her dollars, either bills or gold coins, but their value was very low in those days.

The final link in our food provision chain was Hania. She was a very good homemaker and very economical. Therefore, we were able to manage even when the food situation became increasingly dire.

BATTERIES

One day, Uncle Dziunio came by with a small truck full of flashlight batteries, another product you couldn't get in all of Lwów.

Here again, my buddies helped me sell the goods in various market places.

JOINT VENTURE

Since vodka became a highly profitable product, we decided to make our own.

Wacek was able to sneak impure rubbing ethanol out of the Institute. Our first problem was that it was dyed blue. Luckily Wacek, as a chemist, knew how to distil the alcohol in such a way that he neutralized the color. He did that with the help of the instrumentation he had bought at rock-bottom prices at the school equipment supply store the previous summer.

Hania and I diluted the pure alcohol with water 45:55, so that it had the correct alcohol percentage of vodka, and filled the empty bottles she had bought from the local pubs. To make our product "original", we used a German two-Pfennig coin that depicted an eagle holding a swastika in its claws to make an embossed lacquer seal. This gave our product a somewhat "official" appearance, and it didn't take long until our "moonshine" vodka was sought after, because of its high quality.

POWER SHORTAGES

Since the electrical supply was very poor, Wacek came up with various methods to provide us with light during the constant shortages. Although Father had a French degree in electrical engineering and would have been proud of his son's ingenuity, he didn't agree to all of Wacek's ideas because he was afraid we'd get caught. He didn't want to risk seeing us sent off to a concentration camp.

EXPERIMENTS PUT TO PRACTICE

One of the methods used to store power was to charge nickel-cadmium batteries – normally used in schools for physics experiments – to power light bulbs.

Our charger was enormous. It was the size of a small table. Wacek attached it to a one-foot high lamp. During charging, this bulb produced light – and made a lot of noise.

CAN'T BE CHOOSY

Later on, we used a small 12-volt lamp that stood on our dining room table. When there was no electricity or the Germans didn't allow us to use it, we would turn that lamp on and sit around it to be able to read or do homework.

It didn't give too much light, but it was better than nothing. When you compare our charger to modern day ones, which are the size of a pack of cigarettes, it is easy to understand how tedious it was to charge batteries in those days.

OUTSMARTING THE SYSTEM

Since we were only allowed a limited amount of electricity, Wacek came up with the idea that if we switched the wires of our electric meter, it would run backwards and therefore reduce our measured usage.

So every evening, after the curfew, he switched the wires. It was a rather dangerous endeavor, because the electricity meter was located outside our apartment on the staircase and someone could see what we were doing and denounce us.

HEAVY-DUTY METHOD

To turn the meter back as quickly as possible and reduce the risk of getting caught, we used different heaters and other power-consuming appliances.

We had to make sure that we didn't turn the meter back too far or it might indicate we didn't use any electricity at all – or in the worse case, have a lower reading than we had the previous time.

These were our daily little adventures, but you still had to watch out that you wouldn't get caught and penalized.

HARRASSING BREAKS

A very annoying German invention were the imposed electricity breaks, meaning that there was, in fact, electricity, but we weren't allowed to use it.

During these breaks, inspectors came by to check on us to make sure we complied with the restriction. If someone was caught using electricity during such a forced break, they were fined at a very high rate or had to pay the inspectors bribes, which often weren't much cheaper.

ANOTHER POWER TRICK

To counter this new problem, Wacek came up with another solution.

There was only one wire out of three phases that went through the meter. He took the other wire and connected it with the ground wire to a 220-volt transformer. This way, we used electricity for light, but the power usage didn't show on the meter.

SHORTAGE OF GAS

The pressure of our gas was often very low, and sometimes so low that it wasn't enough to cook with. Wacek came up with the idea to use a suction pump which he bought – where else? – in his beloved school supply store on Akademicka Street. He attached the pump to the kitchen sink faucet. When the faucet was turned on, the running water sucked gas thereby increasing the gas pressure to the extent that allowed Hania to cook dinner.

DEFYING THE ENEMY

Trying to look like a gentleman

These things may sound very simple and unimportant today, but in those days it was one of the important means with which we defended ourselves against our enemies.

SOCIAL OPPOSITES

Going back to my business school buddies, I would like to point out Romek Hryniewicz and Bolek Mucha – mucha is a "fly" in Polish.

Bolek was 3–4 years older than I and a typical "Batiar", i.e., someone from a section of Lwów where mostly blue-collar workers and poor people lived; except that he was always very well dressed and a successful businessman making a lot of money on the black market.

Me, Bolek Mucha and Romek Hryniewicz

MYSTERIOUS MUCHA

Mucha wasn't interested in education, but was in school only to have the obligatory papers. He always laughed and was a good friend. He loved to make fun of me for being from the upper class which was an unknown world to him, but at the same time he was eager to learn as much as possible about how people like us lived before the war.

BUSINESS MATTERS ONLY

He was my good customer and sometimes we went through the park for a walk to talk and "inhale fresh air" as he liked to say.

I had no idea where or with whom Mucha lived. He never talked about his personal life.

STRANGE HABIT

What I remember of him is that when he came to school and passed the soup kitchen run by the nuns, he tore open the door and shouted nasty things at them, before slamming it shut and racing up to the second floor where we had our classes.

.

UNUSUAL CAREER CHOICE

Mucha's good friend was Romek, son of a male midwife. After his mother died, his father married again. His stepmother didn't like him and there were always problems with Romek.

Romek liked to threaten to move out. His father asked him how he thought of supporting himself on his own. Romek responded that he would become a male prostitute. That was a very shocking idea in those days.

LWÓW GHETTO

In the meantime, the Germans set up a Jewish Ghetto in Lwów. It was situated in the old city, in a section where poor Jews had lived before the war.

Since our school was near by, we often saw Jews walking outside of it when they went to work closely guarded by Ukrainian police.

CONCENTRATION CAMPS

We heard about Jewish arrests and about the concentration camp on Janowska Street where most of the Jews were held.

Szymon Wiesental lived there and later wrote about life there in his memoirs. Janowska was also a transit camp. There was also another part of the camp where non-Jewish people were held before they were then sent to forced labor in Germany.

STORIES OF HORROR

There were stories about Germans murdering Jews outside the city in a place they called "the Sands". The city's supply of sand came from these pits.

There was a lot of gossip and many bizarre tales about what was going on there. We couldn't imagine that the Germans were capable of such evil and cruelty, but later learned that they were actually true.

SHORT-RANGE RADIOS

The first thing the Germans did when they invaded Lwów was to order us to give up all radios that had a range beyond the city limits. We were only allowed to listen to our local station or we could use it as an amplifier for our record player.

LONDON CALLING

Father spent many evenings with Professor Weigl, who, due to his status, had permission to have a long-range radio with which he could listen to foreign stations.

But even he, if he got caught listening to enemy stations, risked the death penalty.

SENSE OF IRONY

The Professor lived within the confines of the Institute. The entire terrain was guarded by soldiers of the German army and you couldn't get into it without the proper papers. It is difficult to understand why Father and the Professor felt safe enough to listen to the BBC knowing that the enemy was always there and just a few meters away.

One logical answer lies in the fact that there were different kinds of soldiers. There were those who worked there to avoid service on the Eastern front. They didn't want to create any problems, because that would have increased their chances of being moved from the Institute to the battlegrounds to defend Germany at the gates of Moscow and Stalingrad during the Russian winter.

SPREADING THE NEWS

Father fortunately had a great memory, so all the news he got from London, he immediately passed on to his friends, either in the coffee shop or at home.

Many people came to our house to hear the latest news. Even though he tried to be very careful, Father's love for political analysis was always stronger and he didn't miss an opportunity to talk about WWII-related politics.

He was really lucky that no one reported him to the Gestapo, because in that case his life and that of the Professor's would have ended tragically.

UKRAINIAN BRUTALITY

I will never forget the day that I was walking on Saint Sophie Street to Stryjski Park. I saw a street car coming down the street from the fairgrounds. In the front, there was an open platform full of Jewish workers. When the street car came to the corner, to the front of the school for blind children, it derailed and people standing on the platform fell off and onto the street pavement. Many of them were bleeding.

The moment that happened, the street car immediately stopped. The Ukrainian police present jumped off it, surrounded the men, and started to hit and kick them. They didn't care that the people were injured; all they were worried about was that someone would escape.

NEWS FROM THE UNDERGROUND

The day that Poland was cut up and obliterated from the map in the 18th century, Poland's underground press was born and has continued to flourish in bad times.

Wacek always brought home the latest underground information. Just like the others, we read the papers and passed them on very fast so a maximum number of people had access to them.

Since Father always provided us with the latest news from London, the underground press didn't offer us any revelations. We were more interested in the local news and the latest rumors which generally were distortions of the truth.

MR. KOCH

Back when Father owned his car import business, which included a car repair garage, he employed a few good mechanics. One of the best was a German named Koch. When Father had to close his business, Koch took over the repair shop which he ran for a few years.

I don't remember why, but the fact was that the take-over wasn't too friendly, and they parted on bad terms. One day, during the German occupation, Father walked down the street and saw Koch – wearing an SS uniform. They greeted each other, but I am not sure they talked. In any case, this encounter left Father very uneasy.

THE PAST THAT HAUNTS YOU

Just as under the Soviets, old grudges could easily be accounted for under the new occupying forces.

Father was not politically involved, but he was a member of the hunter's society and of the rifle association, which was an organization of patriotic Poles who practiced shooting and were there to help the army in case it was needed.

All an SS-man like Koch would have to do is drop a story or two about my father, say that he was anti-German etc., and the following night, his buddies would come and take Father away.

Father remained nervous, but somehow nothing happened. He was grateful that Koch never used his status to get retribution and must have considered their unresolved issues as done and over with.

SKIS, WINTER CLOTHES, WHAT NEXT?

In the fall of 1941, if I remember correctly, the Germans ordered us to either hand over our skis or destroy them. The possession of skis was as of then illegal.

Shortly after that, they confiscated fur coats and warm boots. You had no choice but to comply, because you never knew what could happen to you if they caught you in the streets with these prized possessions.

As we didn't want to accommodate the Germans in any way, my skis were chopped into pieces and burned. I don't remember what Wacek did with his own, much better skis. Mother's fur coat was much too elegant for soldiers fighting in Russia and I think we weren't required to surrender it.

MEANWHILE, ON THE FRONT

German troops arrived in front of the gates of Moscow, but then got stuck. In spite of their big announcement that there would be a big parade on Red Square, nothing happened.

A FISHY PLAN

My school friend Staszek lived outside the city. In front of his house was a pond in which we swam and kayaked during the summer in the old days.

That was until the Soviets came and took over the pond to store live fish. The good thing that came out of it was that Staszek's brother, Zdzisio, became the manager of the fish farm. When the Germans took over, the situation remained the same, except that it was no longer run by the State, but by a privately-owned German company.

With Christmas approaching, and according to Polish tradition, it was essential to have carp for the holidays, so I made a deal with Zdzisio to "privately buy" fish from him for my family and friends.

CARP BUSINESS

A few days before Christmas, I took my sleigh on which I had tied a small wash tub. I loaded the fish into it and returned home. There, Hania helped me move the slippery fish into the family bathtub. Hania brought a scale which I set up on a chair.

Then, I opened my shop. People came and selected their fish. It took quite some effort to catch, kill, wrap and weigh the fish, but considering my profit, it was worth it.

This became a seasonal job I did for several years. That way, we always had carp and I made some extra pocket money. Zdzisio also profited from this business deal, since he backhandedly siphoned the fish from the Soviets and later the Germans, and thereby, had an additional income as well.

EAU DE COLOGNE WILL DO IT

As soon as the bathtub was empty, I unplugged the water and put the scale back in the kitchen. I tried to get rid of the fishy smell by using a lot of cologne. This made the room smell even worse for quite some time. Nevertheless, I can say that the project was successful and the income was quite good.

That is how I became a fishmonger, even though I hated to cut and clean these slimy creatures. But I kept reminding myself of the Romans saying "Pecunia non ole" meaning that money doesn't smell, so I managed to overcome my revulsion.

MY SHOP

I guess one can say that I officially opened my "shop" at home the day Germany declared war on the Soviet Union when I loaded up on goods bought with my savings. First, I sold Soviet cigarettes, and, later, I added pencils, ink, note books and other school supplies I bought in the stationery store across the street before they ran out of merchandise.

During the following summer school break, when store business was low and their prices were still the same as during the Soviet occupation, I took advantage and stocked up. When the school year started and the stores quickly sold out, my customers started to roll in. My best client was my friend Wiluś, who had money and could not get supplies. The other one was Leszek.

ICE RINK CLOSED AGAIN

Since it was no longer possible to go skiing, we went skating instead. But our nearby skating rink on Pełczyńska Street became again inaccessible to pedestrians. The building across the street that once housed the NKVD office was now occupied by the Gestapo. In addition, you weren't allowed to walk on that side of the street anymore. So we went to the other rink that was farther away.

Staszek Brunarski, Janka and me

SWEET JANKA

That winter I visited my friend Staszek quite often. The main reason was because I was in love with his sister, Janka. She was two years older, short and had dark hair.

From time to time, she spent time with us to keep us company. Sometimes she brought along her girl-friends as well, when they didn't have any older boys to hang around with.

Janka and me

FORCED TO HIDE

Staszek's mother was Jewish and this increasingly became a problem. One day, she decided it would be best for all if she went into hiding in one of the cloisters. She remained there until the end of the war.

Staszek's parents were quite wealthy. Their house was full of precious objects and they had several servants. With her mother's departure, Janka increasingly felt like she was the new mistress of the house and began to boss the domestic staff around.

PERFIDIOUS PLOT

During one of my visits, one afternoon in the midst of the winter, there was a knock on the door. A man's voice identified himself as the Ukrainian police and ordered us to open the door. Since Staszek's father felt anxious and it was something about his wife, he obeyed.

He opened to the door to three armed men who announced this was a robbery. They rounded all of us up and threatened us if we didn't follow their orders.

I secretly took off my watch that was very precious to me and slid it into my sock. Fortunately for me, nobody was interested in us kids.

Curiously, the robbers knew exactly where the valuables were and what they wanted. They ordered us to put the selected items on the floor. That done, they took as much as they could carry. They warned us not to leave the house for the next ten minutes. They said they would be watching and would shoot us if we disobeyed.

They said a few bad things about Jews while waiting for their horse carriage to arrive. After they loaded everything into it, they left.

TIME OF THE VULTURES

I have to say I was scared and this experience left me with a lasting shock which took me a long time to get over. Sadly, this was not an unusual situation, for many places were robbed.

.

The police in those days were only interested in solving political problems, and we weren't sure if the police and the thieves hadn't collaborated in the break-in. One indicative clue was the fact that the men were Ukrainian police. They were known to pursue their own private business after getting off their shift. The Germans tolerated such actions, as long as they didn't cause any problems for them.

GETTING CAUTIOUS

After this incident, I reduced the frequency of my visits to Staszek and instead insisted he come to visit me. And also I was afraid they might have more problems with the Germans, because of their mother's Jewish background, her hiding and the fact that Staszek and Janka were half-Jewish.

ADAPTING TO THE CIRCUMSTANCES

To be frank, I don't have too many memories about the rest of the school year. The international situation was very depressing and we didn't see an end to the war.

Our biggest concern was not to get caught by the Germans. If something dangerous happened, we split up by going in different directions and ran as fast as we could.

GERMAN NEWSREELS

The summer of 1942 was rather peaceful. We went on bicycle trips and we went swimming in the flooded clay pit.

From time to time, Germans showed newsreels at the market place not far from our house. I remember going there once or twice. Since we didn't go to the movies anymore, it was at least something quite interesting to watch.

Shortly after the failed landing of the allied troops in Dieppe, German propaganda was very happy to show how they conquered and killed the landing troops and humiliated the miserable Canadians they managed to catch.

RUN!

During the presentation somebody suddenly screamed "budy". This was the warning call that German round-up trucks were approaching. The Germans habitually approached their victims by surprise, rounded them up, loaded them into tarp-covered trucks and drove them to the camps, or straight to one of the execution spots.

When someone shouted that word, everybody started to run and hide wherever they could. In these moments, all you relied on were your instincts.

Wacek and I ran home as fast as we could and never looked back. Until today, I don't know if there actually was a round up or if somebody just made a bad joke. It was not possible to find out, because nobody asked questions. Nobody wanted to create any waves.

It was fifty years later when I finally saw the landing in Dieppe – in a documentary on the History channel.

TICKING TIME BOMB

Upon my return to school, things returned to the same manner as the year before. The only difference was that we increasingly talked about the fact sthat in eight months, we would no longer have our papers. We were concerned about finding a place to work in order not to be deported to Germany, like my half-Jewish friend, Rysio Grundman.

RYSIO GRUNDMAN

Rysio's mother was Austrian and his father was Jewish, but Rysio and his brother Henio were baptized in the Catholic

Church. Moreover, Rysio attended St. Joseph Catholic School which is where we met.

During the German occupation, he, his brother and his father were forced to live in hiding. At one point, Rysio couldn't bear it anymore psychologically and volunteered to be sent to Germany to forced labor.

Rysio wrote me heartbreaking letters from Germany. The work he was forced to do was so hard, it was beyond his physical capabilities. Even though he nearly died of exhaustion, he wasn't allowed to return.

Tragically, he died when the factory he worked in was bombed by the Western allies.

His mother died of cancer, but his brother Henio and his father were saved. After the war, they changed their name and worked in the oil industry in Poland, until 1968. That's when an infamous wave of Communist-inspired anti-Semitism struck Poland. By then, Henio had enough of discrimination and harassment, and emigrated to Sweden, where he still lives today.

LICE ARE THE ANSWER

I started to talk to my father about my immediate future. As a result, he arranged an internship at the Institute where I would learn how to become a "lice dissector". This was the person who dissects the lice's gut to extract the Rickettsiae bacteria, needed to make the typhus vaccine. As soon as school ended, I would start to work there as a normal employee.

I was satisfied with father's plan and continued to study. During that time, I increasingly worked as an underground press messenger, well knowing that if I was caught I would be sent to a concentration camp in the best case, or more likely shot.

ANNUAL RITUAL

Before Christmas 1942, I bought fish from Zdzisio again and became the holiday fishmonger. That year, I sold more fish and, lucky for me, there was a shortage of fish so prices went up, and I increased my profit considerably that year.

9. (1943–44)
CHANGE OF THE TIDES – PART TWO

STALINGRAD

The Germans were trying to conquer Stalingrad, but instead of gaining a victory to which they had grown accustomed, they couldn't advance. The Russians started to counterattack with fresh soldiers. The situation began to deteriorate for the Germans.

At the end of January 1943, the Germans permitted the Polish welfare association to organize a big concert in the former Atlantic Movie Theater in Lwów. The proceeds were intended to finance their various aid projects for poor people.

We received official permission to go. So after almost three years of a complete absence of culture, meaning concerts, theater or cinema we were eager to see a real performance with great artists from Warsaw and beyonds.

UNSUSPECTED TURN

It was very difficult to get tickets, but somehow we managed to get lucky and we were really looking forward to seeing the performance. A day before the date, the Germans surrendered to the Soviets in Stalingrad. To mourn their defeat, they closed all entertainment venues – including our theatre.

We didn't share their sorrow, but we were just as sad. To make things worse, there was no alternative date for a new concert. So our hope to grasp a wisp of cultural wind evaporated.

JOINING THE WORK FORCE

Just as Father planned, in February I went to the Typhus Institute twice a week to train for my new job. The manager of the department was a small lady with a lot of patience. She was very nice to me and taught me how to cut up the dead lice.

First, you made a tiny cut behind the third leg of the louse. With one hand, you made an incision with a special small knife while you held the louse's body using a needle with the other hand. All this was performed on a lit piece of glass under a 30x-magnification binocular microscope.

BE NIMBLE, BE QUICK

It was something that was possible to learn, but since the daily norm was 1600 lice in six hours, you had to have a lot of experience before you could be hired as a regular employee.

I didn't have much choice. I wanted to get an "Ausweis", the I.D. with the German eagle on it. We preferred to call it a crow.

"Lice Dissector" at the Typhus Institute - taking a break

LIGHT IN THE TUNNEL

Between school and work, I didn't have too much time left for leisure. Moreover, the Germans were rounding up and arresting more and more people. Private social meetings were the only thing we could do more or less safely. In school, I only had my few buddies to socialize with.

Otherwise, I hung around the group of Hania Czekanowska. She had a lot of girl-friends and invited boys of proper standing to her place. I went to her parties where we played different games and often danced. This is where I made my first innocent attempts at flirting.

KATYŃ

In April 1943, the German media announced the discovery of mass graves in the Katyń Forest and gleefully pointed a finger at the Soviet Union who adamantly denied the massacres.

About 12,000 officers were taken prisoner during the 1939 Soviet invasion of Poland, the rest were Poles who were arrested for being „an enemy of the State", which included most policemen, landowners, factory owners, lawyers, priests, and officials. An estimated 22,000 Polish military officers, policemen, intellectuals and civilian prisoners of war were murdered in the Spring of 1940.

It was only in 1990, half a century later that the Soviet Union, under Michael Gorbachev, finally admitted to have committed this atrocity, as well as the subsequent cover-up. From the moment we heard the dreadful news, we had no doubt that this was a Soviet crime. We hadn't forgottens what they had done in the Brigidki and other prisons in Lwów just before they fled the city.

Among the Katyń victims were the husband of my first cousin Wanda Szybalska, as well as Uncle Luniewski, husband of my Aunt Renia. We were in contact with him until April 1940. The revelation of the brutal mass murders was very depressing and German propaganda took advantage of every opportunity to exploit our anger in order to woo us to join the German side.

The day I learned about Katyń

This picture was taken for my Typhus Institute "Ausweis" made out by the "Oberkommando des Heeres". On my way to the photographer, I passed an open-air market on St. Sophie square – the place where we had watched the German Wochenschau about the failed landing of the allied troops in Dieppe – when the discovery of the mass graves in Katyń was announced over loud speakers.

LOSING GROUND

After the Soviet victory at Stalingrad in February 1943, the Soviet army remained on the offensive. Under pressure from his generals, Hitler agreed to the attack on Kursk the following summer.

He didn't know that his intelligence about the Soviet position had been undermined by a concerted action of misinformation. The battle cost Hitler over 500,000 troops and 1,000 tanks, and was seen as a turning point in Germany's war efforts on the Eastern front.

UNFORGETTABLE TRAIN RIDE

Before I started to enter the work force, I went on a two-week vacation during which I visited Uncle Dziunio and his family in Warsaw and I later went to Końskie to see my Godfather.

The trip alone was an experience in itself. First of all, all non-Germans had to travel tightly squeezed in the few train cars they permitted us to occupy. In the front part of the train, the Germans traveled very comfortably in spacious cars.

FRIENDLY FIRE ENCOUNTER

When we passed through partisan territory, the German cars were shot at by guerrillas, probably Home Army soldiers. At that moment, we were happy that we weren't sitting in the front cars. We heard people screaming. Germans rushed into our full cars and tried to hide among us. At the next stop, two ambulances were already waiting to rush the injured Germans to the hospital. I don't know how the story ended, because there was no one you could ask. As always, the gossip factory went into overtime and sputtered a lot of wishful thinking.

NOBODY HOME

Uncle Dziunio lived in a nice area, called Fort Mokotowski, in a house with a fenced in garden. I walked up to the entrance and rang the bell, but nobody answered. I grew increasingly upset, worrying that soon the curfew would start and I didn't have a place to go. I couldn't go to my other uncle, because it was too far away to get there in time. Besides, they weren't expecting me and might not be home.

WRONG PACIA

Later, I found out that when I rang the bell, my family was manipulating the electric meter. That's why the door to the garden was locked. One of them peeked out the window and saw me wearing my Tyrolean hat. Because the last electrical power plant inspector wore the same kind of hat, they mistook me for him. Everybody froze inside and waited for me to leave. It was only when they heard my tearful whining "But this is me! It's me" did they realize who I was and finally opened the door.

BEFORE THE UPRISING

In the Spring of 1943, Warsaw was a very dangerous place to be. The underground was very active. And so were the Germans. They were catching people all the time and sending them either to German labor camps or keeping them as hostages in order to publicly execute them on the streets as retribution for any attacks against Germans. You could find their bloody traces on almost every corner in the city. The Germans often stuffed plaster of Paris into their victims' mouths so that they couldn't scream "Long Live Poland!" or "Poland will not succumb!" before they were gunned down.

ILL AT EASE

I felt very uncomfortable in this powder keg of mortal tension, and since I didn't know my way around Warsaw, I didn't dare go anywhere on my own. I restricted myself to just a few visits to my large family.

In the country, at Uncle Zygmunt's, the situation wasn't much better. Many houses were being robbed, either by bandits or the Communist "People's Guards". Just as my uncle who had barely had anything left in his home. Whenever he had something, he was immediately robbed. This was not only unpleasant, it was also very boring. Just like our trip to his estate in Malachów. To get there, we had to drive through the forest which was under control of the Polish Home Army (A.K.) partisans. It was the first time I actually got to see the men I had heard so much about. But they weren't very entertaining either. After I sat out the allotted time, I was only too glad to return home.

GOLD MINE FLOUR MILL

Under German occupation, farmers were obliged to deliver a compulsory amount of grain to the Germans. If they wanted to mill excess grain, they needed special permission. As Uncle's flour mill was located deep in a forest that was full of partisans, the Germans were afraid to enter. Because of this situation, Uncle's mill became a real "gold mine". It became the place where farmers could mill without permits – of course at an additional price. Since the safety of the mill was due to the presence of Home Army soldiers, Uncle shared the profit with the Polish Home Army.

INTO THE FUTURE: TRAGIC ENDING

When this open secret became known to the Soviets after they reoccupied Eastern Poland, the Polish Communist Secret Police came to Uncle to arrest him and confiscate his profits. Since most of the money had been given to the Polish Home Army, there was not too much was left.

Unsatisfied with what they got, they tortured him and beat him so severely, that he died of a kidney injury shortly after his release.

PRUDENCE PAYS OFF

Immediately upon my return, I began to work at the Weigl Institute. In the morning, I finished the last days of school and in the evening I dissected lice on the second shift.

After I received my diploma, I told the school director that I already had a job. Thanks to father's foresightedness, he didn't have to report me to the employment office.

WHITE LIES WITH RED LICE

The work in the Institute was quite pleasant. I spent six hours every day staring at enlarged lice, and I learned to adjust to the job.

A colleague revealed to me that I didn't really have to dissect 1600 lice per day, but actually only 1300 or even just 1200. All you had to do was to warm the receptacle containing the gut extract with your hands. That would increase its size and look like 1600. This trick was used for the vaccine for the German Wehrmacht. Only the containers we prepared for Professor Weigl, i.e., for the Polish/Jewish underground use, had to contain the correct amount.

MAXIMIZING MY OUTPUT

With time, I got better and faster and could fulfill my quota in just fours hours. I used the remaining time to socialize with my colleagues.

When the weather was good, we would go out to the botanical garden which bordered the Institute during our breaks. Most of the time, I wandered around, sometimes we played football, but the breaks weren't that long so we didn't have time for much else.

Taking a break in the botanical garden. Me in my lab coat (left).

Me (left) between the girls

HELPING HANDS

Various romances began in this garden, so there was always something to talk about later during work. I was again the youngest in our group, but there were a lot of people who looked after me. In the beginning, they helped me make my quota. Later, I paid them back by being there for them when they needed help.

One of my good acquaintances was Krysia. She lived on St. Marek Street as well and was working with me in the Institute. We went to work together and sometimes for walks in the park. She was very pretty, two years older than I and had a fiancé whom she married, but later divorced. She died recently. I learned a lot about the Underground and was impressed by how many people were involved in it. I volunteered when they needed additional help, even though it was very dangerous.

Krysia and me

GUARDED TRIPS

Since most of the employees were young people, we often went on trips to go swimming or kayaking on the weekend. Once we went to Janów, a big lake not far from the city. To get there, we had to go by train which at that time was not always safe, because the German police loved to arrest people on trains.

Someone told our German Institute guards about our plans. These guys had grown to like us and were afraid we'd run into problems with the Ukrainians. The guards decided to send two German soldiers to accompany us – just to be on the safe side.

Excursion to Janów (I'm the second one on the right)

KILLING FOR POLISH I.D.S

For those who had sided with the Germans, the situation was becoming increasingly critical. Everybody was talking about the German retreat and the so-called liberation by the Soviets. It was the time when Ukrainians increasingly murdered young Polish people in order to get their identification cards so that they could change their identity in case the Germans lost the war.

POLISH UKRAINIAN TENSION

The Typhus Institute had two locations: The main building was located in the old university where Professor Weigl also lived, and the other part was situated in the former high school of Queen Jadwiga (Hedwig). Across the street from it was a Ukrainian Police Station. The two parties hated each other, even more so as our people knew that they were collaborators protected by the Germans.

The employees from the Institute often teased the Ukrainians and their constant anti-Ukrainians jokes further heightened the tension.

SS GALICIA

However, as soon as the Germans formed the "SS Galizien" division, the Ukrainian police started to become more self-assured. For them, Germans were Übermenschen (Superhumans) and thus earned their respect.

A few years ago, I watched a 60-Minutes report on CBS that showed Ukrainians who had served in the SS and were presently walking the streets again in their uniforms, proudly displaying their decorations – in Lwów, of all places!

The commentator pointed out that Lwów, now a part of the western Ukrainian republic, was the only city where SS uniforms can be worn in public.

UNDERGROUND SCHOOL

According to the Germans, I officially reached the end of my scholastic education with the end of the school year. I was only 15 years old. According to the Germans, this was the end of the schooling rope for Poles. Nevertheless, Father decided that I should continue my education.

The only possibility we had in Poland was to go to an illegal underground school. We talked as little as possible about this secret, because, in case one of us would be caught, we wouldn't know enough to endanger the others involved. As of the beginning of September, I was free during mornings to go to the underground school since work on the second shift didn't start until the afternoon.

HOW CONVENIENT

"Going" to the underground school is an exaggerated term, because the classes were held directly in our house.

My class consisted of three people. Sitting next to me was my friend and neighbor Zbyszek. He was a few months older, but already an orphan. His mother had died a long time previously and his father was murdered by Ukrainians. He was taken in by his aunt, the sister of his father, who lived with her husband and child in our house one floor below us, in the apartment Professor Czekanowski and his famous 50-kilo bag of sugar once occupied.

PITRALON AFTERSHAVE LOTION

When not in class, Zbyszek worked in a drugstore on Akademicka Street. Even though I couldn't shop there, because it was "nur für Deutsche" (only for Germans) he sold me Pitralon, an aftershave lotion I liked to use now that I was beginning to shave.

Decades later, when I stayed at the Kempinski Hotel in Berlin and went window shopping down the famous Kurfürstendamm, I discovered a bottle of Pitralon in a bathroom gift basket in a store display. That surely brought back a lot of memories. I bought a bottle, but when I smelled it before I splashed it on my face, I didn't like the smell anymore. I didn't use it, and left the bottle in the hotel.

LOOSE ENDS

My friendship with Zbyszek ended when I left Lwów. I don't know what happened to him and so far I haven't been able to contact him.

ROMEK

The third student in our illegal class was Romek. He was as old as me. He couldn't attend classes on Saturday, because he had to help his father in his barber shop. Zbyszek and I often laughed imagining how Romek practiced by shaving cream off a glass bottle because this is supposedly how you learned to shave back then.

UNDERGROUND RULES

People who attended an underground school were not allowed to carry any papers, books or notes, so that in case they were stopped and searched they wouldn't have any evidence of a conspiracy on them.

OUR CLASSROOM

We did our best to make "our classroom" – which consisted only of my old desk – look as normal as possible and give it a school-like atmosphere.

CHEATING

All three of us had difficulties in Latin, but I seemed to be unable to get even one word into my head. The only way I survived was that I used a trick. Since it was my desk, I got to sit behind it.

As the teacher stood on the other side, he couldn't see the little cheat sheets I had hidden under it. That may not have improved my Latin, but at least I had a lot of fun.

LEARNING RESULTS

I attended underground classes from September 1943 until March 1944, when we had to leave Lwów.

Did I learn anything under such conditions? Of course I did. Maybe not as much as in a normal school, but I didn't have a choice. Anyway, I didn't miss any time and, what was most important – I was moving forward.

RICKETTSIA PROVAZEKI VARIANTSI

Every Institute employee had to be inoculated against typhus before starting to work there. Nevertheless, some of us got infected by some less harmful variants of Rickettsia provazekii, the bacteria that causes typhus.

When I was affected by what was called "zakładówka" or quintana, I had a very high fever and was shaking to the point that I was physically jumping. It was so bad, I was losing my balance. Then, I was overwhelmed by a splitting headache and heavy vomiting. This continued for twelve hours. I thought it would never stop. The doctor from the Institute quickly came to my home and gave me several vaccine shots. After several days, I slowly recuperated.

DIZZY SPELLS

Until this day, I have problems dancing because of that shock. I can't dance the waltz, because I can't turn in circles. When I do dance, I can only make one full turn, then I have to turn in the other direction. Otherwise, I get a dizzy spell and a headache.

Nowadays, I don't even think about it anymore, since I've worked out those 180-degree to-and-fro turns in my special style...

EUROPEAN KNOWLEDGE

Exactly 50 years later, I had another attack. Gratefully, this time it only lasted fours hours. I was lucky that my doctor was a German lady who understood what I was talking about. She had learned about my situation a few years prior and therefore, knew how to treat me: She gave me the right medication and I recuperated fairly quickly.

So far, I haven't met an American doctor who knows what my disease is.

10. (1944–1945)
POWER PLAY PAWN

BRUTAL REALISM

In the beginning of 1944, Father, who was very well informed, now had to acknowledge that his pessimistic predictions sadly turned out to be true. He understood that our western allies weren't going to oppose Stalin's plans to take over eastern Poland and that Lwów would become a part of the Soviet empire.

It was very difficult to accept that America and England were helping Stalin and even worse, that we wouldn't receive help from the so-called allies who had officially guaranteed the sovereignty of our borders.

Since we had no intention to greet these so-called liberators in Lwów and become Soviet citizens again, we decided to leave Lwów and move to Central Poland.

DECISIONS FROM HIGH UP

We didn't know at that time that soon after, we would have had no choice but to leave our hometown and go into forced exile.

At that time, there hadn't been any word yet about the "repatriation" of Poles. That meant that we were to leave what was now defined as Soviet territory and move to western Poland which had been taken from the retreating Germans. This was stipulated in a secret agreement first between Hitler and Stalin in 1939, then reemerged in Teheran, later confirmed at Yalta, and finally written in stone at the Potsdam Conference.

The American and British governments treacherously agreed to these facts behind the backs of the Polish people.

PREPARING FOR EXILE

Since the frequency of robberies had further increased, thereby making his life in the countryside impossible, Uncle Zygmunt had moved to a large rented room in Końskie.

In February 1944, Father went to see him and rented a place for us there. Upon his return to Lwów, he rented a small truck. We loaded a few mattresses, some personal things, including family portraits, art objects and silverware into it, as well as us: Mother, Babcia, me and our dog, Czyki.

LEAVING LWÓW

Father sat up in front with the driver. We said good-bye to Lwów, the town where I was born and grew up. We also parted from Wacek, who stayed behind to finalize his studies and graduate from the Technical University (Politechnika Lwowska) before joining us in Końskie a few months later. We sadly bade farewell to our faithful cook and beloved friend, Hania, and left for an unknown future.

Our first stop was in Lublin. Along the way, we were stopped several times by Germans and Polish Home Army partisans, but as we had proper documents they had to let us go.

In Lublin, we parted with Babcia who stayed there with her family. The plan was that her son, my Uncle Dziunio would come from Warsaw and pick her up.

WRONG DECISION

We had no idea that it was to be our final good-bye with Babcia. Uncle Dziunio explicitly put his mother in a retirement home for old ladies of society, run by nuns because he was worried that he would not be able to take care of her during the impending Warsaw Uprising in which he was going to take part. Moreover, he believed that she would be much safer there.

Nobody could have expected that during the Uprising, Babcia's retirement home would be stormed by a group of Cossacks whose commander was former Soviet officer

Kaminski and was now under German command. They let the nuns go, but then murdered all the old ladies and set the residence with their corpses on fire.

Only by chance did I learn from a co-worker several years later, the horrible truth about my grandmother's tragic ending.

KOŃSKIE

The next day, we arrived in Końskie and started to live in our new location where we stayed a year, until the end of the war. Our new "home" could only be accessed through the attic. It consisted of a small room, in which Father slept, and two adjoining attic spaces; Mother slept in one, and I and Wacek shared the other when he later joined us.

Since we lived under the roof and the ceilings were slanted, we often hit our heads. There was no water or bathroom. An outhouse was located outdoors, in the middle of a large garden. Going to the toilet wasn't much fun, especially in the winter when there was snow. And we had a lot of snow that winter.

Compared to our beautiful apartment and house in Lwów, this place was very depressing. We always admired our mother who never complained. She also never said a word when she moved to Sopot where, after Wacek did not return from his scholarship in Denmark, we were forced to accommodate three families in our apartment.

She was a real lady.

EPILOGUE

To leave Lwów, the town where I was born and raised, where I spent my childhood, was very, very sad. However, there was a war still going on, and I was much more concerned with its horrors than thinking about my childhood and what I was leaving behind. There was no possibility to go back. Our life in Lwów had ceased to exist.

The shock hit me much later when our lives were stabilized in new surroundings. That's when I really became aware that we had lost more than our home, and that was my beloved Hania.

The new environment and conditions were so different and much poorer than those I had known before. A new life began and we had to accept it. I started to think of leaving Poland and to emigrate. This idea took shape when my brother emigrated to the States and wanted me to join him. But this was during the last years of Stalin's reign of terror, so that I was temporarily forced to abandon this dream.

My luck changed a few years later, when Stalin's death brought about an amelioration of life behind the Iron Curtain, and I was finally able to emigrate and join my brother. The most impressive moment for me was when the SAS plane with me on board took off from Warsaw's Okêcie airport and I was on my way to a free world, a place about which I had dreamed and yearned for so many years.

Fourteen years passed before I returned to Poland again. A few years later, I visited Lwów. My former hometown had become a totally different place than the one which I had left in 1944 – 34 years earlier.

If I had arrived in Lwów directly from America and had not been familiar with post-war life in Eastern Europe, and especially in the USSR, I probably would have been devastated. But since I'd had been traveling through Communist Europe for seven years on business, and had spent several months in Moscow, I was well adjusted and better prepared to see what had happened to the place and home of my childhood.

In Lwów, I went on several tours with local guides as a "tourist". It made me sick to hear the lies they told. But that was the time, when it would have been dangerous to express my feelings, so I forced myself to keep my mouth shut.

Four years later, my entry visa to the USSR was revoked and I ceased to exist for all my local friends. It took me seven years and Perestroika to let me get back into the Soviet Union, but by that time there was no more business for me. Soon after, I retired and moved to Florida where I spent my first American Christmas.

What impressed me the most there was that I could walk in short sleeves to midnight Mass, instead of being dressed in coat and boots and having to walk through the snow.

My first car

Szybalski Reunion in Wisconsin (1963): Mother, my nephew Stefan, me, my niece
Basia, my sister-in-law Elisabeth, Wacek, my daughter Eva and my wife Louise

APPENDIX A: PEOPLE

MY FAMILY ON 2 MAREK STREET

Me   Stanisław Szybalski

Mother   Michalina Szybalska (née Rakowska)

Father   Stefan Szybalski

Wacek   Wacław Szybalski
my brother

Babcia   Stanisława Rakowska
my grandmother

Hania   Anna Stojanowska
our housekeeper

Kasia   Katarzyna Jagielska
Babcia's companion 1939-1941

SZYBALSKI

Uncle Zygmunt   Zygmunt Szybalski
my uncle and godfather, Father's brother

Uncle Bronek   Bronisław Szybalski
my uncle, Father's oldest brother

Aunt Cesia   Cecylia Szybalska
wife of Bronek, mother of Wanda and Lalunia

Wanda
my first cousin

Wanda Szybalska

Lalunia
my first cousin

Marysia Szybalska

RAKOWSKI

Uncle Dziunio
my uncle, Mother's brother

Tadeusz Rakowski

Aunt Jagoda
wife of Dziunio, mother of Renia

Jadwiga Rakowska

Renia
my first cousin

Teresa Rakowski-Harmstone

Uncle Bogdan
my uncle (his great-grandfather and my great-great grandfather were first cousins)

Bogdan Rakowski

ARCISZ/KRÒLIKOWSKI/CZEMINSKI

Ujcia
my aunt (my great-grandmother and her grandmother were sisters)

Ujcia Arciszowa

Uncle Tadzio Arcisz
husband of Ujcia

Tadeusz Arcisz

Jurek
Ujcia's son

Jerzy Arcisz

Mancia   Maria Królikowska
Ujcia's oldest sister and my godmother

Uncle Żuś   Stanisław Królikowski
Mancia's husband

Wacek Królikowski   Wacław Królikowski
my cousin

Aunt Kazia   Kazimiera Czermińska
my aunt and wife the director of the Sea and Colonial League

BOGDANSKI

Leszek   Aleksander Bogdański
my cousin and friend

Aunt Zosia   Zofia Bogdańska
my aunt, Leszek's mother

LASOCKI

Dr. Wacław Lasocki
Co-founder of the Nałęczów spa, my great-grandmother's brother

DOBROWOLSKI

Tadzio   Tadeusz Dobrowolski
my cousin

Babcia Taborowska
Uncle Tadzio's grandfather's sister

FRIENDS and ENCOUNTERS

Aunt Janka   Janina Raczkowska
Mother's good friend

Manusia   Maria Mościcka
second wife of Ignacy Mościcki, the third President of the Second Polish Republic, Mother's good friend

Marysia Różycka
artist

Kasia Różycka
airplane pilot

Mr. Gołębiowski
house painter

Janitor Janek   Jan Dobrzanski
house janitor

Krysia Jasińska
Wacek's girl-friend in the summer of 1939

Ewa Jasińska
my first girl-friend in the summer of 1939

Jurek Michotek
Wacek's classmate, and later famous singer

Dr. Mehrer
urologist

Dr. Gruca
orthopedic surgeon

Professor Groer
pediatrician

Tadeusz Tadeusz Boy-Żeleński
gynecologist, pediatrician, poet, literary critic, and university professor of French literature under soviet ocupation. He was murdered in July 1941 during the Nazi occupation of Poland in what became known as the massacre of Lviv professors.

Professor Rudolf Weigl
Polish biologist and inventor of the first effective vaccine against epidemic typhus and director of the Typhus Institute, Lwów. In 2003, he was awarded by Yad Vashem as Righteous among the Nations.

Hans Stuck
German-Austrian racecar driver, winner of the 1931 Grand Prix in Lwów

Rudolf Caraciolla
German racecar driver

Janek Ripper
Polish racecar driver, physician and Father's friend

NANNIES

Ziunia
Polish nanny

Fila
German nanny

Elza
German nanny

Emma
German nanny

Mila
Polish nanny and maid

SCHOOL TEACHERS

Mr. Gryksztas

Brother Bonawentura

Brother Grzegorz

Brother Anzelm

CLASSMATES

Rysio   Ryszard Grundman
half Jewish, half Austrian

Staszek   Stanislaw Brunarski
half Jewish

Janusz   Janusz Krysa

Adaś	Adam Chlipalski
Wiluś	Jerzy Wilimowski
Roman	Roman Wêgrzyn
Dziubek	
Sowiński	
Szczurowski	
Szabajko	

FRIENDS DURING THE WAR

Romek	Romek Hryniewicz
Mucha	Bronisław Mucha
Janka	Staszek Brunarski's sister
Zdzisio *fish farm manager*	Staszek's brother
Hanka	Hania Czekanowska
Krysia	Keysia Kubikowna
Zbyszek	Zbyszek Koening

POLISH HEROES

Marszał Piłsudski
Józef Klemens Piłsudski (5 December 1867 – 12 May 1935)

Polish statesman; Chief of State (1918–22), "First Marshal" (from 1920), and leader (1926–35) of the Second Polish Republic. From mid-World War I he had a major influence in Poland's politics, and was an important figure on the European political scene. He was the person most responsible for the creation of the Second Republic of Poland in 1918, 123 years after it had been taken over by Russia, Austria and Prussia.

General Sikorski
Władysław Eugeniusz Sikorski (May 20, 1881 – July 4, 1943)

Polish military and political leader. During the Second World War, Sikorski became Prime Minister of the Polish Government in Exile, Commander-in-Chief of the Polish Armed Forces. In July 1943 the most prestigious leader of the Polish exiles was killed in a plane accident. The exact circumstances of his death have been disputed and have given rise to a number of conspiracy theories surrounding the crash and his death.

General Anders
Władysław Anders (11 August 1892 – 12 May 1970)

General in the Polish Army and later in life a politician with the Polish government-in-exile in London.

Anders was in command of a cavalry brigade at the time of the outbreak of World War II. The Polish forces were no match for the larger and better equipped German Wehrmacht with their massive Blitzkrieg tactics and were forced to retreat to the east. During the fighting and retreat Anders was wounded a number of times. He was later taken prisoner by Soviet forces and was jailed, initially in Lwów and later in Lubyanka prison in Moscow. During his imprisonment Anders was tortured.

Shortly after the attack on the Soviet Union by Germany on 22 June 1941, Anders was released by the Soviets with the aim of forming a Polish Army to fight alongside the Red Army. Continued friction with the Soviets led to the eventual exodus of Anders' men – known as the Anders Army – together with a sizeable contingent of Polish civilians via the Persian Corridor into Iran, Iraq and Palestine. Here, Anders formed and led the 2nd Polish Corps, fighting alongside the Western Allies, while agitating for the release of Polish nationals still in the Soviet Union.

Anders was the commander of the 2nd Polish Corps in Italy 1943–1946, capturing Monte Cassino in the Battle of Monte Cassino.

After the war the Soviet-installed communist government in Poland in 1946 deprived him of Polish citizenship and of his military rank. Anders had, however, always been unwilling to return to a Soviet-dominated Poland where he probably would have been jailed and possibly executed, and remained in exile in Britain. He was prominent in the Polish Government in Exile in London and inspector-general of the Polish forces-in-exile.

Tadeusz Kościuszko

Andrzej Tadeusz Bonawentura Kościuszko (February 4 or 12, 1746 – October 15, 1817) Polish military engineer and a military leader who became a national hero in Poland, Lithuania, Belarus, and the United States. After fighting on the American side in the American Revolutionary War, he designed and oversaw the construction of state-of-the-art fortifications, including those at West Point, New York. Returning to Poland in 1784, Kościuszko was commissioned a major general in the Polish–Lithuanian Commonwealth Army in 1789. Two years after the Polish–Russian War of 1792 had resulted in the Second Partition of Poland, he organized an uprising against Russia in March 1794.

The defeat of the so-called Kościuszko Uprising led to the Third Partition in 1795, which ended Poland's independent existence for 123 years. In 1796 pardoned returned to the United States. A close friend of Thomas Jefferson, with whom he shared ideals of human rights, Kościuszko wrote a will in 1798 dedicating his American assets to the education and freedom of U.S. slaves. He eventually returned to Europe and lived in Switzerland until his death in 1817. The execution of his will later proved difficult and the funds were never used for the purpose he had intended.

POLAND UNDER SOVIET OCCUPATION

NKVD

The Soviet People's Commissariat for Internal Affairs or secret police.

About 500,000 Poles were arrested and imprisoned before June 1941 (when Hitler's Germany invaded the Soviet Union), including civic officials, military personnel and other "enemies of the people" like the clergy and the Polish educators: about one in ten of all adult males. In 1940 and the first half of 1941, the Soviets deported a total of more than 1,200,000 Poles in four waves of mass deportations from the Soviet-occupied Polish territories, while in Western Poland the Nazis and their collaborators murdered ethnic poles who opposed German rule.

Katyń

Originally the term "Katyń massacre" was a series of mass executions of Polish nationals carried out by the the People's Commissariat for Internal Affairs (NKVD) under Stalin in April and May 1940. An estimated 22,000 Polish men were murdered in the Katyń Forest in Russia, the Kalinin and Kharkiv prisons and elsewhere. Of the total killed, about 8,000 were officers taken prisoner during the 1939 Soviet invasion of Poland, another 6,000 were police officers, and the rest were arrested Polish intelligentsia the Soviets deemed to be "intelligence agents, gendarmes, landowners, saboteurs, factory owners, lawyers, officials and priests". The Soviet Union claimed the victims had been murdered by the Nazis, and continued to deny responsibility for the massacres until 1990, when it officially acknowledged and condemned the perpetration of the killings but refused to classify this action as a war crime or an act of genocide.

POLAND UNDER GERMAN OCCUPATION

Edelweiss Battalion

The 1st Mountain Division was an elite formation of the German Wehrmacht during World War II. It was created on 9 April 1938 in Garmisch Partenkirchen from the Mountain Brigade and consisted mainly of Bavarians and some Austrians.

The 1st Mountain Division fought in the Invasion of Poland as a part of Army Group South. On 30 June 1941, the division captured Lwów. There, the Germans discovered several thousand bodies of prisoners who had been executed by the NKVD, as they could not be evacuated. As the news spread, a large-scale anti-Jewish pogrom broke out, in which the town's Ukrainian population participated, stirred up in part by German and 'Organization of Ukrainian Nationalists' posters and proclamations calling for revenge against the "Jewish Bolshevik murders".

Polish Home Army (A.K.):

The Armia Krajowa was the dominant Polish resistance movement in WW II in German-occupied Poland. Its allegiance was to the Polish Government-in-Exile, and it constituted the armed wing of what became known as the "Polish Underground State"

Communist People's Guard (G.L.)

Gwardia Ludowa was an underground armed organization created by the communist Polish Workers Party in German occupied Poland with sponsorship from the Soviet Union. Gwardia Ludowa was created on 6 January 1942 with military aid from the Red Army and was incorporated into the communist Armima Ludowa (Army of the People) on Soviet order in 1944.

Nightingale Battalion

Before World War II nationalist Ukrainians in Galicia regarded Hitler's Third Reich as the only force capable of facilitating the establishment of an independent Ukraine in Galicia, free of Soviet or Polish rule. When in 1939 the Soviet Union occupied eastern Poland, various nationalist groups set up military units to fight the Soviet Red Army. One such was the "Nightingale Battalion". End of June 1941 they took part in a three-day massacre of the Jewish population of Lwów.

SS Galizien

The 14th Voluntary Division SS Galizien was created in 1943 when Nazi Germany were suffering growing losses in the war with the USSR to take part in regular combat on the Eastern Front. The Nachtingal brigade, which was later incorporated into the SS Galizien.

OTHERS

Jan Czekanowski
Internationally renowned scholar of African ethnology and a physical an-thropologist who taught at the Jan Kazimierz University (UJK) in Lwów.

Liza Czekanowska
Jan Czekanowki's wife and Zorka's mother.

Zorka Czekanowska
Wacek's Puppy Love

Hulimka Family
wealthy land owners

Emilia Margerita Gorgonowa
accused murderer

Elżbieta Zarembianka
sixteen-year-old daughter of a successful architect murdered in Brzuchowice

Agopsowicz family
owners of pension in Skole

Monika Agopsowicza
grand daughter of the above

General Orlicz Dreszer
chairman of the Sea and Colonial League

Renate von Natzmer
woman who was beheaded because she helped Polish spy Jerzy Sosnowski

Jerzy Sosnowski
Polish Army officer and a Polish spy in Germany

Karl May
German writer, very popular among older children

Kozak
Communist killed in Lwów during a Communist demonstration

Mr. Koch
Father's car mechanic, later joined SS or SD

APPENDIX B: PLACES

LWÓW

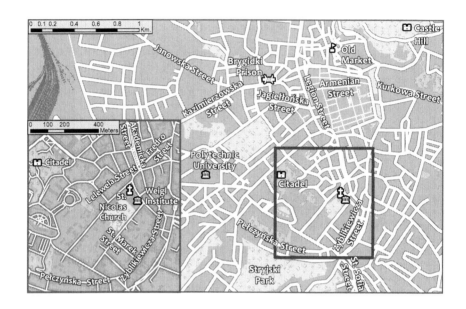

Streetmap of Lwów

St. Marek Street   15, 19, 146, 208

Akademicka Street   20, 94, 163, 178, 212

Stryjski Park   33, 46, 49 ff, 61, 184

Lelewela Street   58

Armenian Streets   73

Fredro Street   109

Zyblikiewicza Street   119

REGIONS

COUNTRIES

Norway (Narvik)   145

Romania (Brasov-Polana)   63, 77

Soviet Union (Moscow, Stalingrad, Kursk)   123 f, 128 ff,
139, 142,152 f, 170, 188, 200, 221, 230 f

Spain   31, 84

Syria   77

Yugoslavia   77

APPENDIX C: MAPS

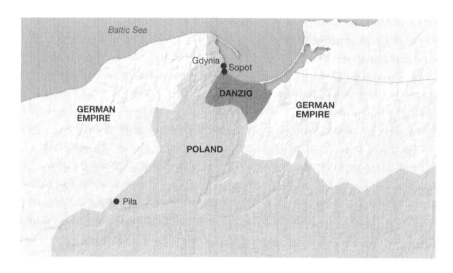

Poland after 1919

Poland in 1939

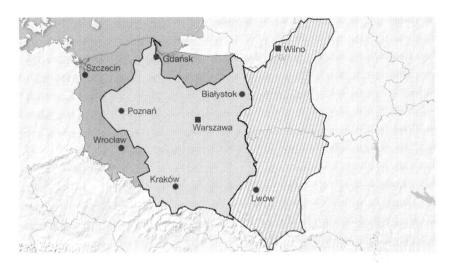

Redrawn Polish Borders in accordance with the decisions made by the Allies at the
Potsdam Conference of 1945 due to insistence of Josef Stalin

Legend:
Dark Grey: German Territory given to Poland,
Striped Area: Polish Territory annexed by the Soviet Union

ABOUT THE AUTHOR

Eva Szybalski, daughter of Stanisław Szybalski, was born in New York City. Now she lives in Berlin where she works as a screenwriter, playright and TV producer.

Find out more about Eva Szybalski on her website:

http://www.eva-szybalski.com/

COPYRIGHTS

The photogaph "View of the city of Lwów from the High Castle Park at sunset" was used and printed in this book with the permission of the photographer Elena Suvorova through Fotolia.

The photograph of "Marshał Piłsudski" (1930) was used and printed in this book, because it is in the public domain. Its copyright has expired and its author is anonymous.

The streetmap of Lwów was used and printed in this book with the permission of the creator Kyle Pipkins.

The maps of Poland were used and printed in this book with the permission of the creator Marcela Polgar.

YOU HAVE REACHED THE END OF THIS BOOK

Did you like to follow Stanisław into his memories by reading "Lwów - A City Lost"?

Then please help us and the author and leave a review for this book in the online-shop/on the platform where you have bought it. You can also send us an email and tell us, what we can do better next time or what you liked best. Therefore please use our mail-address: feedback@if-ebooks.de

if eBooks

http://www.if-ebooks.de/

Printed in Great Britain
by Amazon